A DAILY
DEVOTIONAL

FOR THOSE IN THE
WORKPLACE

MON**D**AY
memos

MARK BILTON

Called to Business Press
45 Lawson Parade,
St Ives NSW 2075 AUSTRALIA
Telephone +61 2 99880956
www.CalledtoBusiness.com

Cataloguing in Publication Data:
Title: MONDAY Memos. A Daily Devotional For Those In The Workplace / Mark Bilton
ISBN: 9780987339829 (paperback)
ISBN: 9780987339836 (ebook)
Subjects: Religion and Theology, Business and Economic
Dewey Number: 248.4

Title Logo by Siah Design
Interior design by Justine Elliott - Book Layout Guru
Images © Olly – Fotolia.com

"I have not stopped giving thanks for you, remembering you in my prayers. I keep asking that the God of our Lord Jesus Christ, the glorious Father, may give you the Spirit of wisdom and revelation, so that you may know him better. I pray that the eyes of your heart may be enlightened in order that you may know the hope to which he has called you, the riches of his glorious inheritance in his holy people, and his incomparably great power for us who believe"

(EPH 1:16–19).

CONTENTS

Introduction 1

January 3

February 34

March 62

April 93

May 123

June 154

July 184

August 215

September 246

October 276

November 307

December 337

About the Author 368

Recommended Resources 369

ACKNOWLEDGMENTS

This is a daily devotional to be read, obviously, every day. The one who truly ministers to me on a daily basis is my loving and ever-patient wife, Helen. She is my greatest blessing after Christ Himself.

To my Lord and Savior Jesus, the Hound of Heaven who lovingly and persistently pursued me into the kingdom and literally saved my life, I am and always will be eternally grateful.

He is my daily bread, and in Him is fullness of joy.

INTRODUCTION

There is a move of God happening all around the world. Its expression is diverse and varied, and it is being orchestrated by the Holy Spirit Himself. It seems to have little structure, with no organized leadership, yet it is impacting people, communities, and nations all over the globe.

"I believe one of the next great moves of God is going to be through the believers in the workplace."

—Billy Graham[1]

The move is one borne out of a frustration with an ineffective model that has closeted and constrained Christians to expressing their faith almost exclusively on Sundays. We have segmented and separated our faith into the religious guise of 'sacred.' We have deemed everything else in life to be secular and ensured that the two are distinctly partitioned. The separation of secular and sacred has rendered us ineffective in reaching those around us and impacting our communities.

The concept that God is vitally, passionately, and intimately interested in our workplace, our business, or our place of employment and industry is completely foreign to most of us. However, people have become more aware of the need for change and have embraced the biblical concept of our whole lives being impacted by God in recent years. The Marketplace Ministry Movement and Business as Mission are two expressions of an awakening that is occurring across Christendom.

This devotional has been written to encourage those who want to see God move in their workplaces, whether they are employers or employees. It seeks to understand and illustrate the areas in our work that can be impacted by our relationship with

---

1   *Faith@Work Movement*, Os Hillman, 2004, Aslan Publishing Group.

God. It seeks to answer the simple yet profound question: "How do I integrate my faith into my work?"

My desire is to see business people all over the world released into the freedom and knowledge of God's plan and purpose in the workplace. With revelation and empowerment, potential is released and dreams are realized. God has a plan and a purpose for your life, and it has been my experience that, without exception, we are all anointed and appointed for a specific purpose.

JANUARY

1

Work before the Fall

"The Lord God took the man and put him in the Garden of Eden to work it and take care of it." (GEN 2:15)

What was one of the first things God did for man? He took man and put him in a place where he was supposed to work. This was not an act of slavery or a consequence of the fall. This was before sin and not a consequence of our fallen state.

God placed man in the perfect place so he could work. Here in this pure world that was uncorrupted and unspoiled by sin, God called man to work. Work is from God and a good thing. It is ordained by a Creator who knows what is important for us. He created a garden that needed some work to be done and knew that it was good for man to work.

Work is not a curse; it is a gift of God.

QUICK PRAYER:
I acknowledge that work came from You, not from the curse.
Amen.

God's Plan

"'For I know the plans I have for you,' declares the Lord, 'plans to prosper you and not to harm you, plans to give you hope and a future.'" (JER 29:11)

Is God interested in our work? If He has a plan for our lives, I am sure it would include the place where we spend most of our time. Do we really think His plan is just for Sundays?

He plans to prosper us and give us hope and a future. How could He prosper us if He were not interested in what we do at work? He has every day planned for us, and that was done before we were even created.

You don't need to wait for Sunday to experience His love and attention. You can walk and talk with Him today and every day at work. His plans for your work are to prosper you and not to harm you and to give you hope and a future. Why not invite Him into your workplace today?

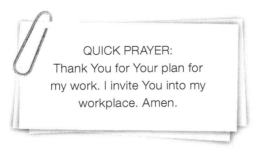

QUICK PRAYER:
Thank You for Your plan for
my work. I invite You into my
workplace. Amen.

JANUARY

3

Money

"For the love of money is a root of all kinds of evil. Some people, eager for money, have wandered from the faith and pierced themselves with many griefs" (1 Tim 6:10)

This scripture is often misquoted as saying, "Money is the root of all evil." The verse in question is correctly quoted above. Money is neither good nor evil. It is a morally neutral tool that can be used for good or to cause damage.

Money buys freedom of choice and options to give and sow into the work of the kingdom. What is it in you and your business that constrains the wanton pursuit of profit at all costs? Greed is moderated by giving; God calls us to a generous life—a giving life—as demonstrated by His Son, who gave His life for all.

The pursuit of wealth for wealth's sake will bring with it collateral damage in other areas of life if it is not counterbalanced with a generous spirit. Moderation is a virtue, and God's principles of giving and sacrifice bring balance to our natural tendency for greed.

QUICK PRAYER:
Lord, please bless my
workplace and balance my life
with generosity and wisdom.
Amen.

JANUARY

4

Reconciliation

"All this is from God, who reconciled us to himself through Christ and gave us the ministry of reconciliation: that God was reconciling the world to himself in Christ, not counting people's sins against them. And he has committed to us the message of reconciliation." (2 COR 5:18–19)

What is it to have a ministry in reconciliation? When we preach in church, we minister to a very small minority. When we demonstrate and communicate our faith in the marketplace, we are impacting a majority. If we are to see a significant move of God, with multitudes saved, it will be because we have taken the gospel out of the church and into the real world.

Bring reconciliation to your family, business, staff, management, industry, and marketplace. Demonstrate ethics and generosity, go the extra mile, take the time to share your faith, and impact your environment for good. The Holy Spirit will empower you and guide you as you serve Him and His purpose in your call to business.

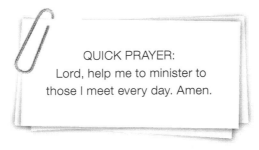

QUICK PRAYER:
Lord, help me to minister to
those I meet every day. Amen.

JANUARY

5

Do You Have 20/20 Vision?

"Then the Lord answered me and said, 'Record the vision and inscribe it on tablets, that the one who reads it may run.'" (Hab 2:2 NASB)

A key part of leadership is demonstrating and constantly communicating vision—not vision as in foresight but vision as in a clearly articulated picture of the desired future. Without a clear vision, your team will be disparate, pulling in many directions. With a clear vision, unity will prevail. Effort will be concentrated on a desired future state.

All levels of your business can benefit from understanding where you want to go. True leadership releases people with empowerment, but without a clear vision, that is not possible. Unless we all know where we are going, we can't do our part to get there.

Jesus gave a clear vision statement just before He left: *"Go into all the world and preach the gospel to all creation"* (Mar 16:15). That is what it is all about. Jesus then empowered us with that mandate and resourced us with the ultimate helper, the Holy Spirit. Surely we should emulate this model in our businesses.

QUICK PRAYER:
Lord, give me Your vision
for my business, and help me to
communicate it clearly. Amen.

JANUARY
6

Can Your Company See Clearly?

"No longer do I call you slaves, for the slave does not know what his master is doing; but I have called you friends, for all things I have heard from My Father I have made known to you." (JOH 15:15 NASB)

Openness and transparency—are they a question of culture and leadership style or a spiritual mandate? Control is often an illusion. Those who are too controlling move people from commitment to mere compliance and often to passive if not overt resistance.

Openness, transparency, and free communication come with a set of risks, which are far outweighed by the trust and positive productivity they engender. Engagement to a clear vision and open communication are a powerful cultural mix.

Innovation, creativity, customer service, and productivity are all increased in an environment of trust and empowerment. If people don't know what's going on, they will make it up anyway; they might as well talk about what is really happening.

QUICK PRAYER:
Jesus, help me to open up and
be secure in You and more open
with others. Amen.

JANUARY

7

The Art of Delegation

"You will surely wear out, both yourself and these people who are with you, for the task is too heavy for you; you cannot do it alone." (Exo 18:18 NASB)

Are you working long hours, tired, irritable, and not spending enough time with your family? This is not compulsory for success. God has said that His burden is light and that He has come so that we may life—life to the fullest.

God will provide you with the resources you need to accomplish the task He has set for you. Are there people in your business you are not delegating to? Do you need to be across all that detail? Can you not trust those around you? If your view is that if you want something done, you have to do it yourself, then stop because you are on the road to trouble, both for yourself and for those around you.

Look at what you have to do, and give away all you can. If you trust others to deliver, you may well be surprised at the outcome—in a good way.

Be very clear on your desired outcome. Make sure your employees are well resourced, and let them loose. You may well be unlocking their God-given talent. The people you always wanted may already be with you.

QUICK PRAYER:
Lord, help me unload what You
never intended me to carry. Amen.

In the Beginning

"God blessed them and said to them, 'Be fruitful and increase in number; fill the earth and subdue it. Rule over the fish in the sea and the birds in the sky and over every living creature that moves on the ground.'" (Gen 1:28)

God called us to work from the very beginning. Work's intrinsic value is not determined by whether it is set in a secular or sacred environment. It is sacred because it is ordained by God. In our modern Christian culture, we have a heretical hierarchical view of vocations. Priests, pastors, missionaries, and monks are all sacred callings, followed by the serving vocations of nurse, teacher, etc. Merchant bankers, politicians, and lawyers reside further down the scale. This is a cultural bias, not a God-given one.

God values a call to business as any other call. A sacred vocation is made sacred because it is mandated by God. He uses it to fulfill His purpose in our lives and calls us to serve in a way that is in line with His way: virtuous, ethical, and with excellence, "as if serving the Lord."

QUICK PRAYER:
Thank You for the validity of my
calling. Thank You for work.
Amen.

JANUARY

9

No Calling Is above Another

"Each one should retain the place in life that the Lord assigned to him and to which God has called him." (1 COR 7:17 NIV1984)

Martin Luther wrote, "A cobbler, a smith, a farmer, by means of his own work or office must benefit and serve every other, that in this way many kinds of work may be done for the bodily and spiritual welfare of the community, even as all the members of the body serve one another."[2]

We are called to stay more often than to go. Doing what you do is the basis of your service to God. He will use you where you are, change you where you are, and grow you where you are. We need to learn to see the sacred in the seemingly ordinary to appreciate God's plan for our lives.

As we submit in this, the motivation will come, the fruit of the Spirit will be manifested, and true ministry will begin to occur.

> QUICK PRAYER:
> Lord, thank You for where You
> have planted me. Help me to
> see You in all I do. Amen.

---

2   Martin Luther, "An Open Letter to the Nobility," in Donald Bheiges, *The Christian's Calling* (Philadelphia, PA: United Lutheran Church in America, 1958), 53.

A Word of Encouragement

"And we know that in all things God works for the good of those who love him, who have been called according to his purpose." (Rom 8:28)

We serve the God of the breakthrough—the God of the impossible! There is nothing you are facing today He was surprised by. He has the answer, and in many cases, it is already on its way. Please don't try to cope on your own. Invite Him into your problems, small and large. Sometimes you will get an instant miracle and other times a slow recovery.

Occasionally we are put under pressure to produce fruit, change, and be molded in the furnace. We can face these things in the knowledge that He loves us and that all things work together for good for those who love Jesus.

QUICK PRAYER:
Lord, help me to understand
Your will in this situation and to
pray accordingly. Help me in my
time of need. Amen.

JANUARY
11

We Walk a Fine Line

"Watch out!...a man's life does not consist in the abundance of his possessions." (Luk 12:15 NIV1984)

How easy it is to be distracted with work, wealth, and possessions. Trust Jesus to cut through and tell it like it is. We need to be reminded of our priorities and of the things that can so easily ensnare us. Our life is more than what we do, where we work, and what we own. We are called to operate with excellence in our sphere of influence yet be untainted by its falsehood.

Jesus again exhorts us in Matthew 6:33 to *"seek first the kingdom of God and His righteousness, and all these things shall be added to you."* Our challenge is to run our agendas, schedules, focus, efforts, and resources on His mandate and His priorities. Only then will we truly be operating in excellence and building His kingdom.

QUICK PRAYER:
Lord, show me Your schedule
and priorities for my life and
business. Amen.

JANUARY
12

A Warning to Those around Us

"What good is it for a man to gain the whole world, and yet lose or forfeit his very self." (LUK 9:25 NIV1984)

Growth is good and optimizing profit a spiritual mandate. But the unfettered pursuit of wealth brings a warning from God. To those around us, meaning is derived from the accumulation of possessions, but Jesus once again tells it like it is. Even if you were to become a billionaire or have the wealth of nations, it is of no value if you lose your very soul.

Our calling is to demonstrate this to those around us. The wanton pursuit of wealth is only moderated, contained, and augmented by a loving God working on the spirit of man, moving us from glory to glory as we are being transformed into the likeness of Him who gave His life for us. This is not by our works but by His unmerited favor and grace.

QUICK PRAYER:
Jesus, keep me from greed,
and help me to demonstrate
Your grace to those around me.
Amen.

JANUARY
13

Counting the Cost

"For which one of you if he wants to build a tower, does not first sit down and calculate the cost, to see if he has enough to complete it?" (Luk 14:28 NASB)

How in touch are you with your business finances? Do you know what your 'break even' will be on that upcoming project or new product? How is your cash flow, that vital air that keeps your business alive? What is the real bottom line by product line or customer?

So many great businesses have grown quickly and then died, simply by not counting the cost. You can easily outgrow your cash flow and get into trouble. If you are entrepreneurial like me, you will be emotionally attached to that new product, service, or business idea. Get the advice you need to truly count the cost. Take a calculated risk, not a stab in the dark.

A little time to assess risk and suitable funding requirements can make the critical difference between success and failure.

QUICK PRAYER:
Help me to count the cost with
wisdom. Amen.

Diligence and Personal Growth

"Be diligent to present yourself approved to God as a workman who does not need to be ashamed." (2 Tim 2:15 NASB)

How is your skill level? Have you, like a lot of leaders, neglected your own development to serve your company? Diligence is not only applying yourself to your duties with vigor; it is also ensuring you are advancing and growing. If you look after yourself, you will often have more to give others.

Do not neglect reading, learning, listening to wisdom, attending a seminar, or meeting together with likeminded businesspeople. Be diligent in your own growth and development and everyone around you will benefit. When that happens, you can present yourself to God as a workman who does not need to be ashamed.

Invest in yourself, and you will see a return that will bless those around you.

QUICK PRAYER:
Lord, help me to help myself
and grow in wisdom and
knowledge so I may serve You
with diligence. Amen.

JANUARY

15

Are You a Promise Keeper?

"It is better that you should not vow than that you should vow and not pay." (Ecc 5:5 NASB)

Our integrity is always demonstrated by what we say. Do we offer more than we can deliver? Do we paint a picture that is overly rosy? Do we dangle a carrot in front of our staff that will be hard to meet? The Scripture says our yes should be yes and our no, no (see Mat 5:37). There is no grey, just black and white.

Sometimes it is not easy to say it like it is. Often when circumstances change, we struggle to meet our commitments. Perhaps we should do what we said we will do and let God sort out the consequences. He will honor a stand that is done in line with His requirements of us.

We can live by the Word of God, keep our promises, and run a successful, growing, profitable, influential business.

QUICK PRAYER:
Jesus, You always demonstrated absolute integrity. Help me to walk like You. Amen.

Do You Value Your Team?

"For the body is not one member, but many." (1 Cor 12:14 NASB)

A successful business is the interaction of many tasks performed by many people. Valuing each member of a team regardless of his or her task or role ensures an inclusive culture and internal communication.

Like any chain, you are as strong as the weakest link. Often the hidden people doing the seemingly mundane are critical to a smooth, effective organization. Public and private acknowledgment of their significance is not only the right thing to do but also produces a wave of genuine productivity.

Do not underestimate the power of taking time to say hello. Encourage and take a genuine interest in the personal life of all your staff, especially those others ignore. You will be amazed at the results.

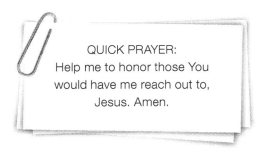

QUICK PRAYER:
Help me to honor those You
would have me reach out to,
Jesus. Amen.

JANUARY

17

How Do You Treat Your Suppliers?

"So the craftsman encourages the smelter, and he who smooths metal with the hammer encourages him who beats the anvil."
(Isa 41:7 NASB)

Now this is an interesting question! Are you brutal and over demanding of those who supply you goods and services? Isn't it a good business practice to extract the last possible cent from those you do business with? The Bible shows us a more synergistic relationship of mutual respect and encouragement.

Long-term relationships built on an understanding of shared profitability can be priceless as cycles move and pricing power shifts up and down supply chains. Building those relationships on respect and going to the extent of encouraging our suppliers is doing business God's way. The very fact that it does not happen very often ensures that you will stand out, become a customer of choice, demonstrate a different approach, and represent the God you profess to serve.

QUICK PRAYER:
Help me to demonstrate Your grace to my suppliers. Amen.

JANUARY
18

Hearing from God 1

"But when he, the Spirit of truth, comes, he will guide you into all the truth. He will not speak on his own; he will speak only what he hears, and he will tell you what is yet to come."
(Joh 16:13)

In order to be effective in our businesses, we need to hear from God. If we are surrendered to Him and recognize His want to be involved in the marketplace, then we should expect His guidance.

Throughout the Bible, people walked and talked with God. They heard instructions, affirmations, discipline, and words from and for others. Some were moved through circumstance initiated by God; others saw angels, dreamed dreams, had visions, or simply received Godly counsel.

If God is the same yesterday, today, and forever, then we should expect to hear from Him. Often He is guiding and leading, directing and initiating, and we are just unaware. However, He is calling us to intimacy, to walk with Him. We need to hear from Him and minister to those around us out of the resources He gives to us.

QUICK PRAYER:
You are Lord of all. I surrender
all I have and all I am to You.
Amen.

Hearing from God 2

"Paul and his companions traveled throughout the region of Phrygia and Galatia, having been kept by the Holy Spirit from preaching the word in the province of Asia." (Act 16:6)

If you have now surrendered or committed your business to God, He will arrange circumstances. Look for coincidences in your day, like unexpected answers or contacts. Look for the seemingly prearranged. Notice also the doors that will not open. Some are to be pushed and others to be left alone. Look of the hand of God. Paul was hindered from going into Asia and took that as God shutting the door.

Listen to the quiet sense of inner peace, the still, small voice in your spirit. Do you feel really uncomfortable about a deal or opportunity? Learn to take note of your sense of peace, both from a positive and from a cautionary view.

God will show you His will in more direct ways as well. You will be amazed at how directly He can guide you. It is no different from the first church and early apostles preaching the gospel in the marketplaces of the Middle East.

QUICK PRAYER:
Jesus, help me to hear from
You. Amen.

Hearing from God 3

"I will instruct you and teach you in the way you should go; I will counsel you with my loving eye on you." (PSA 32:8)

It is almost mind boggling to try and understand why an infinite and almighty God would want to commune with His creation. He does so not as an odd event but on an ongoing basis with those who surrender to Him as Lord.

He will lead and guide you in many ways. A *rhema* word can be a Scripture that really impacts you. If you read your Bible regularly, ask the Holy Spirit to highlight His will for you. Often a verse will almost leap of the page or certainly draw your attention significantly.

Sometimes someone is speaking and you are struck by a phrase of sentence that is highlighted to you. These words are often a final confirmation of a decision of important direction that you already have peace about and the circumstances have all lined up. He can and does speak through prophecy, dreams, visions, and even angels. It's not as crazy as it sounds. We are on an important mission and in a spiritual battle for souls. Don't underestimate Godly people who can bring a word of wisdom born of experience.

QUICK PRAYER:
Jesus, speak to me in my daily
life as I go about the business
You have called me to. Amen.

JANUARY

21

Have You Asked Your Staff Recently?

"Jesus stopped ordered the man to be brought to him. When he came near, Jesus asked him, 'What do you want me to do for you?'" (Luk 18:40–41)

You are in a position of authority, and even if you are accessible, many will be intimidated by your position. If you ask, "What can I do for you?" you give an opportunity to others to respond. It may very well help them do their part in the company.

Often the simple things are forgotten yet can be easily changed or given to adequately resource your people. We all liked to be asked, even if we don't need anything. It shows that someone cares about our opinion.

Jesus is asking us the same question. He is able to change any situation, provide any resource, and meet any need, and He is asking, "What do you want Me to do for you?" Go ahead; ask.

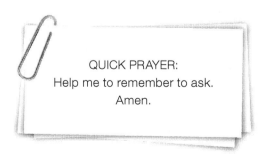

QUICK PRAYER:
Help me to remember to ask.
Amen.

Is God with You in the Ordinary?

Avodah.

Avo...what? Avodah is a Hebrew word that occurs regularly in Scripture. It is at the foundation of all that it is to serve and praise our God. The word is translated as *worship,* and its other meaning is *work.*[3]

Work and worship—could they be the same thing? Your work place is your place of worship. As you serve God in excellence and learn to see Him in all you do, you worship.

Brother Lawrence was a lowly monk in the seventeenth century who practiced the presence of God. He found worship in serving others and doing the simplest of tasks. His letters are now part of the pivotal writings of church history and of how to walk with God at work. His real name was Nicholas Herman, which sounds less spiritual and says more about who he really was. But Nick found he could sense God's presence in the mundane and the menial; that is true worship.

The truth of God doesn't become dated. It is eternal. That work and worship are the same word says it all. Avodah!

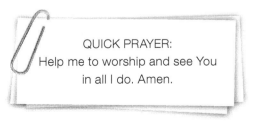

QUICK PRAYER:
Help me to worship and see You
in all I do. Amen.

---

3   David W. Miller, God at Work: *The History and Promise of the Faith at Work Movement* (Oxford University Press, USA, First Edition, 2006), 6.

JANUARY

23

Excellence

"Whatever you do, work at it with all your heart, as working for the Lord, not for human masters." (COL 3:23)

I love excellence. I appreciate seeing things done well, professionally, efficiently, and effectively. A well-conceived idea powerfully executed and delivered is great to experience.

God calls us to strive for excellence by working with all our hearts, passionate and committed. Sometimes that is not easy. In particular we are not to look at our earthly masters. They may be a board, a company owner, a CEO, or whatever. You may disagree; they may be incompetent or inexperienced, rude or overbearing. Regardless of whom you serve, the only way to have the right attitude is to serve them as if you were working for the Lord, worshiping Him.

Keep coming back to this powerful truth; it may well help you overcome immense frustration. It is sometimes not easy, but God's Word will prevail.

QUICK PRAYER:
Guide me into excellence in all I
do as I serve You. Amen.

Do Your Staff Members Know Where They Are Going?

"The assembly was in confusion: Some were shouting one thing, some another. Most of the people did not even know why they were there." (ACT 19:32)

How cohesive is your team? If you asked them to articulate their main purpose or the company's key goals, could they tell you what they were? A creative environment with lots of open opinions should be valued. A culture where differing positions are not only tolerated but encouraged is rare yet desirable. However, a process of decision-making based on specific, demonstrable goals and outcomes, underpinned by clear jurisdictions and authorities, is critical to contain this vibrancy in a cohesive structure.

When you place potential in an enabling structure, there is a synthesis that produces a multiplier effect. Take the emotion, innovation, and creative passion and place it in a structure to guide and channel that power, not one to contain and constrain it. The motivation for structure is as important as the structure itself.

All this has to be undergirded by crystal-clear leadership, sounding a definitive note, bringing an end to confusion of direction.

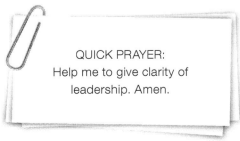

QUICK PRAYER:
Help me to give clarity of
leadership. Amen.

What Is Your "Point of Difference"?

"Even in the case of lifeless things that make sounds, such as the pipe or harp, how will anyone know what tune is being played unless there is a distinction in the notes?" (1 Cor 14:7)

In order for you to be successful, your product or service has to be distinctive. If not, you will only be a "me too," pushed and pulled around by the whims of competitors and locked in a price decrease cycle. There will always be a competitor who unwisely chooses to sell it cheaper.

What is it that you do well? Why do customers choose to buy from you? How can you enhance that difference and make yourself more distinctive? If you have a clear advantage, a point of difference, you can show a reason for a higher price and gain a greater margin whilst increasing your market share. Yes, it is possible. The profitability gained can enhance your competitiveness further by allowing increased development or investment.

Being distinctive and moving away from a commodity mindset is a critical success factor.

QUICK PRAYER:
Jesus, please show me what
makes us distinctive. Amen.

JANUARY
26

Who Is the Boss?

"Whatever you do, work at it with all your heart, as working for the Lord, not for men." (COL 3:23 NIV1984)

We all report to someone: a manager, an owner, the shareholders, partners, a board, and that most insidious of masters, the bank. How do we act when they are not present or not demanding something specific? Do we slack off? Are we disrespectful? Do we only do what is required and no more?

The Bible challenges us to act and work as if we are serving God Himself. This is because in reality, we are working for and with a Savior who has given His all for us. How much more, then, knowing what He has endured for us, should we endure all things and work with all our hearts, serving Him? This should not be out of compulsion but out of a grateful heart.

Not only are we thankful for what He has done but also for what He is doing. There is opportunity all around us when we submit to God in this way. As we serve Him, His purposes are revealed to us.

QUICK PRAYER:
You deserve the best, Lord.
Help me to remember Who I am
working for. Amen.

JANUARY
27

Does Your Product Make a Noise?

"When Athaliah heard the noise made by the guards and the people, she went to the people at the temple of the Lord."
(2 Kin 11:13)

We live in a world of information overload, of white noise, bombarded by a seemingly never-ending push of product endorsement, advertising, and placement. How do we get potential customers to hear? What is more important? How do we get them to understand, and want to buy, our product or service?

To be noticed, we have to be creative. Traditional methods just don't work anymore. Consumers are discerning and educated and have more choice than ever before. There is a rise in social networking and community thought, environmental concerns, individual customization, and exponential technology innovation.

One thing is for sure: there is no shortage of communication. One smart idea and the whole world can hear about it in twenty-four hours. So get praying, get creative, and explore how you can make a noise.

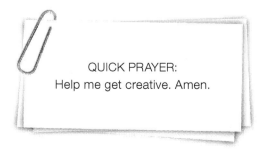

QUICK PRAYER:
Help me get creative. Amen.

JANUARY 28

Counting the Cost?

"Suppose one of you wants to build a tower. Will he not first sit down and estimate the cost to see if he has enough money to complete it?" (LUK 14:28 NIV1984)

This seems like such an obvious instruction, but how often do we leap into something without really looking at the cost? That may be in terms outside a pure financial evaluation. Will this new direction, project, or product take up too much of our existing resources? Does it cannibalize our existing range, for example? Sometimes the unintended consequences can do some damage beyond financial failure.

This Scripture talks specifically about money. Do you have enough financial resources to complete what you are building? Know how much you will need to get the job done; simple advice from a God who cares about you and your success.

If He wants it done, He will provide the resources to complete the task.

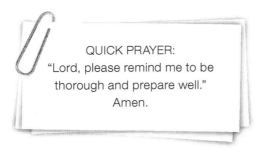

QUICK PRAYER:
"Lord, please remind me to be thorough and prepare well."
Amen.

Do I Communicate Our Vision Well?

"And the Lord answered me and said, Write the vision and engrave it so plainly upon tablets that everyone who passes may [be able to] read [it easily and quickly]." (Hab 2:2 AMP)

Here are some great aspects to how our vision should be presented:

Written: If it is in your head, no one can see it.

Plain: Keep it very simple so that it is memorable.

Everyone: Make it available to all.

Passes: Keep it accessible and in plain view.

Read: Did I already mention written?

Easily: You don't need big words to be credible.

Quickly: Short is good.

How clear is your vision statement, company idea or purpose, or whatever you choose to call it? Test it against the mandate above. There is a lot of Godly wisdom in a plain, simple, easily read, available, clear vision.

God gave us one: "Go into all the world and make disciples of all men."

QUICK PRAYER:
Lord, please give me clarity
and the ability to articulate it
effectively. Amen.

What Does It Take to See the Kingdom of God?

"In reply Jesus declared, 'I tell you the truth, no one can see the kingdom of God unless he is born again.'" (JOH 3:3 NIV1984)

You can only see the kingdom of God if you are born again. This occurs as we ask Jesus to forgive us and make Him Lord over our lives. Our spiritual eyes are then open, and we begin a journey of discovery in the kingdom.

Do you know you are going to heaven? Do you have an assurance that you are born again? You may have been around church all your life but not yet made a full commitment of your life to Jesus. Why not make that decision today? You have a lot to gain.

It is the call of a heavenly Father to His lost children.

QUICK PRAYER:
Lord, forgive me for my sin. I acknowledge Jesus as my Lord and Savior. I give You my life.
Amen.

JANUARY
31

What Belongs to You?

"For from Him and through Him and to Him are all things. To Him be the glory forever! Amen." (Rom 11:36 NASB)

All that we have, all that we are, and all of our opportunities, relationships, and resources have come from Him. In reality, when we take an eternal perspective, all we have is on loan from our beautiful Creator.

We can do nothing of eternal value without Him. As we surrender what He has given us to His purposes, we open up eternal opportunities. It is so easy to be distracted by the pull of all that is around us. While we are called to live life well and enjoy His blessings, our true home is with Him.

Let's hold what we have only lightly, as stewards and faithful servants. Imagine a world where we caught the reality of this truth—where we truly used what we have for the kingdom.

QUICK PRAYER:
Lord, I acknowledge that all I
have and all I am are from You.
Use me for Your glory. Amen.

Does God Give People Wealth?

"But remember the Lord your God, for it is he who gives you the ability to produce wealth, and so confirms his covenant, which he swore to your forefathers, as it is today." (Deu 8:18)

God doesn't give us wealth; He gives us the ability to produce wealth. This speaks to a responsibility of fruitfulness. We have to take the ability and use it wisely, in accordance with Biblical principles. The ability is a gift. The wealth, the fruit, and the responsibility come with not only a command to multiply but in how we use it.

The parable of the talents is often used as an analogy for gifts. The talent was a unit of currency, so this parable is about money. The command is to be fruitful with the resources we are given.

God is interested in our finances and how we create them and use His gifts to build wealth at work.

QUICK PRAYER:
Thank You for the ability to produce wealth. Help me to do it Your way, for Your glory. Amen.

FEBRUARY
2

What Does the Church Have to Do with Business?

"It was he who gave some to be apostles, some to be prophets, some to be evangelists, and some to be pastors and teachers, to prepare God's people for works of service, so that the body of Christ may be built up." (EPH 4:11–12 NIV1984)

The church as an institution that is populated with the fivefold ministries is to prepare you for works of service. The role is to prepare believers for the work to be done outside the church in the marketplace.

The full expression of our work with God is to be manifested in our daily work, not within the four walls of the church. However, it is vital to be well connected to a place of worship where you can be refreshed and prepared as you go out again to minster in the world.

We are called to be "fishers of men," not keepers of the aquarium.

QUICK PRAYER:
I commit to supporting my local church. Show me how I can help. Amen.

Where Is Your Hope?

"Command those who are rich in this present world not to be arrogant nor to put their hope in wealth, which is so uncertain, but to put their hope in God, who richly provides us with everything for our enjoyment." (1 TIM 6:17)

If the global financial crisis taught us anything, it was that wealth is indeed fleeting, uncertain, and not to be relied on for security. We need to put our hope and trust in God. It is He Who is our security, He Who is our salvation, and He Who is our protector and provider.

We should put our trust in the eternal certainties and then see them manifest here. As we grasp less for the here and now, we receive more here. It is a paradox but a heavenly one.

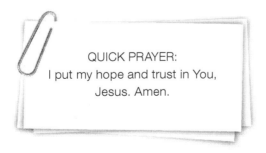

QUICK PRAYER:
I put my hope and trust in You,
Jesus. Amen.

FEBRUARY
4

Where Do You Invest?

"For where your treasure is, there your heart will be also."
(LUK 12:34)

Here is a sobering thought: imagine if God has kept a record of all our checks, automatic payments, and credit card transactions. Could He tell just from those where our priorities are? Where we invest is where our hearts are and shows what we view as important. Our priorities are evidenced by our investments.

If we take an eternal perspective, looking down in a couple of hundred years or so, what would be important? Is it the temporal, instant satisfaction of the latest toy or gadget or perhaps the eternal souls affected by an investment in a mission, a gift, a ministry supported, a church planted, or a soul won?

Even while we work, there are opportunities to operate and invest in the work of the kingdom. There is no place better to demonstrate our priority for the things of God.

QUICK PRAYER:
Lord, show me how to invest in
the kingdom. Amen.

FEBRUARY
5

Eternal Profit?

"Do not store up for yourselves treasures on earth, where moth and rust destroy, and where thieves break in and steal. But store up for yourselves treasures in heaven, where moth and rust do not destroy, and where thieves do not break in and steal. For where your treasure is, there your heart will be also." (MAT 6:19–21 NIV1984)

There is a reward for kingdom investment—a reward with eternal value. As the great song "Amazing Grace" says, "When we've been there ten thousand years…" What a great perspective, for our lives here are so short compared with our eternal lives. The value of what we do, the reward for what we do, how we spend, and where we invest should reflect the temporal nature of our earthly existence.

Our true security is not found in a bank balance and assets but in a relationship with God who has cattle on a thousand hills.

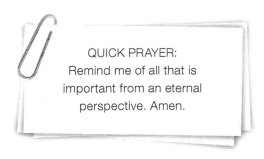

QUICK PRAYER:
Remind me of all that is important from an eternal perspective. Amen.

FEBRUARY

6

Priorities?

"But seek first his kingdom and his righteousness, and all these things will be given to you as well." (Mat 6:33)

Are you chasing after all the worldly stuff, like, "What shall I wear? What shall I eat?" Jesus said, "Don't worry; get busy with what I have called you to do, and I will sort out all that other stuff. Make My work your priority and you won't have to worry about all the things ungodly people fret about."

That is a terrible paraphrase, but the essence is true. As we get our focus on God's priorities, our needs are met by a loving, providing God. He is indeed El Shaddai, the God of more than enough.

At work we are tempted to put away the ways of God and save them for Sunday. The priorities we run our lives by need to be lived and demonstrated seven days a week.

QUICK PRAYER:
Help me to put You first in all I
do. Amen.

Praise You, Lord?

"Yours, Lord, is the greatness and the power and the glory and the majesty and the splendor, for everything in heaven and earth is yours." (1 Chr 29:11)

Take a moment to ponder the infinite splendor of our great Creator, the Maker of the universe and Master of the infinite detail in all around us.

His glory is indeed revealed in the sunrise, the sky, the sea, and the beautiful order of nature. Take a moment to wait in awe of your Creator, who knew you and loved you even before you were knit together in your mother's womb.

Is any problem you are facing too great? Nothing is impossible for God, and He is for you, not against you. When we meditate of His greatness, our problems begin to reveal their true size. Nothing is impossible to an infinite God.

QUICK PRAYER:
Yours, oh Lord, is the greatness
and the power and the glory and
the majesty and the splendor, for
everything in heaven and earth
is Yours. Amen.

FEBRUARY

8

Generosity?

"But who am I, and who are my people, that we should be able to give as generously as this? Everything comes from you, and we have given you only what comes from your hand."
(1 CHR 29:14)

God gives us excess so we will be able to give to others. He is the ultimate giver; He gave His Son. All we have is His. Let's hold onto it knowing that He may have uses for it elsewhere and be faithful as stewards of all He has given us.

Just as He is generous, so He calls us to reflect His nature. As we spend time with Him and are more obedient to His Word and promptings, we begin to be shaped by His character. We ought to be known for our generosity, just as He is. We are a reflection of His nature and character.

QUICK PRAYER:
Help me to hold on loosely to all
that is Yours anyway. Amen.

Integrity

"I know, my God, that you test the heart and are pleased with integrity." (1 Chr 29:17)

Do you ever feel that you are being tested? Are you going to do the right thing? What about that thing that just popped into your head? You know, the thing you know you should really be doing but are reluctant to do?

Do the right thing, and let God sort out what happens next. Let the consequences be what they may, and be obedient to His call of integrity. As we move in obedience, He can release the most unexpected blessings.

Integrity counts. When we have integrity in the small, seemingly insignificant things, we prepare ourselves for being faithful in the larger temptations and challenges. If you feel like you are being tested, it is probably because you are.

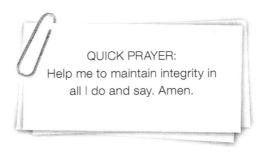

QUICK PRAYER:
Help me to maintain integrity in
all I do and say. Amen.

FEBRUARY
10

Jesus

"For God so loved the world that he gave his one and only Son, that whoever believes in him shall not perish but have eternal life." (JOH 3:16)

This is what it is all about. Familiarity often breeds contempt. Take a moment to read with fresh eyes the familiar words with such a poignant meaning. Jesus made ultimate sacrifice and expression of an incomprehensible love that is so wide, so deep, and so complete that we cannot begin to understand its total, absolute, and monumental enormity.

It is for all history, the perfect expression of perfect love. The enormity of the sacrifice cannot be understood by mortal man or the consequences of rejecting this indescribable gift.

Others need to know what we have heard and experienced. Let the love of others overcome the fear of opening up and letting them know.

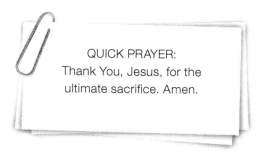

QUICK PRAYER:
Thank You, Jesus, for the
ultimate sacrifice. Amen.

What Is Your Position on Giving?

"Give to everyone who asks you, and if anyone takes what belongs to you, do not demand it back." (Luk 6:30)

It is easy to become paralyzed by the scam artists, the fraudsters, and the false beggars. Soon enough we won't give to anyone for fear of being ripped off or swindled. Jesus had a novel approach: let it go and just give.

I met a great Salvation Army man and asked him about this. His response was, "Sure, use some discernment, but I would rather give to ten and be ripped off by nine if it meant the genuine case was ministered to." What a refreshing view in a cynical world. It is also very much in line with Jesus' suggestion, or was it an instruction? Look for the opportunity to share Jesus' love at work today. There will be at least one.

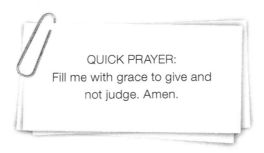

QUICK PRAYER:
Fill me with grace to give and
not judge. Amen.

Been Waiting for an Answer?

"God is not unjust; he will not forget your work and the love you have shown him as you have helped his people and continue to help them." (Heb 6:10)

God has seen your faithfulness. He has seen all you have done and are doing. He will not forget your work. Your answer is coming. Daniel had to wait to see an answer that was dispatched the moment he prayed. We don't understand how it all works or the mechanism of prayer, but we do know He is faithful.

He will watch over His Word to see that it is fulfilled. When we stand in agreement with His Word, we literally pull the promises from the spiritual into the physical. It is in our faith that the answers to prayer are born.

It is because of Who He is that we can count on Him. He is the full manifestation of all it is to be faithful. We put our trust in His character; He is not a man that He should lie.

QUICK PRAYER:
Thank You for your faithfulness
and that You honor Your Word.
Amen.

Need Some Grace?

"And God is able to make all grace abound to you, so that in all things at all times, having all that you need, you will abound in every good work." (2 Cor 9:8 NIV1984)

God will always give you all you need to fulfill His will. It would be very unreasonable to do anything else. Sometimes He will allow us to come to the end of ourselves so that we know we need a heavenly Father and that we cannot do it all in our own strength.

Sometimes I have been in situations where I had no idea what to do and found wisdom. At other times I have been in need of grace toward others and found a new depth of grace and mercy.

He provides what we need, physically, emotionally, and spiritually, to do what He has called us to do.

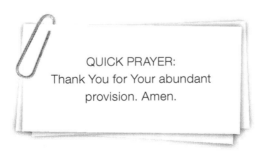

QUICK PRAYER:
Thank You for Your abundant
provision. Amen.

Are You Mature?

"So let's stop going over the basics of Christianity again and again. Let us go on instead and become mature in our understanding." (Heb 6:1 NLT)

There comes a time where we should stop being fed and start feeding others—a time where we become part of the solution. There is infinite depth in an understanding of God. It is an opportunity to commune with a presence beyond our understanding, yet often we settle for so much less.

Let's take the time to move on from the basics and push on to be all we can be. We have a responsibility to ourselves, those around us, and our loving Creator. How often are our prayers a self-interested list of needs and wants? While God does ask us to bring all our concerns to Him, try a prayer time when you only pray for others.

QUICK PRAYER:
Lord, help me to move on from
the basics and be all I can be.
Amen.

Free Ride?

"If anyone will not work, neither shall he eat." (2 THE 3:10 NKJV)

This is an interesting scriptural standpoint on voluntary abdication from responsibility. It also shows us the regard with which God holds occupations and work in general. It talks to the rightful reward of work and the need to apply ourselves to the task at hand.

Our provision, while it comes from God, requires our alignment, surrender, and application to fully manifest. We also need to make sure our attitude is aligned to this principle that work is good.

When we recognize the value of something, it becomes more important to us. God places a high value on our employment and our attitude toward working. It is His mechanism for provision and much more besides.

QUICK PRAYER:
I'm sorry for taking Your provision for granted. Amen.

FEBRUARY
16

Faith Based on Power

"And my speech and my preaching were not with persuasive words of human wisdom, but in demonstration of the Spirit and of power, that your faith should not be in the wisdom of men but in the power of God." (1 Cor 2:4–5 NKJV)

Have you seen the power of God? Have you seen Him move in a miraculous way? In our modern world, He is no less willing to move on our behalf and to demonstrate His power in support of His gospel. Will we dare to believe?

He can demonstrate this in your business. When we invite Him into our workplace and ask big, we have the opportunity to see Him move in mighty ways. When we ask and see Him answer, our faith grows, and we will ask more and for more. He is not reluctant to answer our prayers at work. Why are we so reticent in asking?

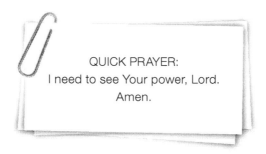

QUICK PRAYER:
I need to see Your power, Lord.
Amen.

Acceptable and Approved

"For he who serves God in these things is acceptable to men and approved by God." (ROM 14:18)

Doing things God's way doesn't necessarily put us at odds with those around us. Sometimes we assume that we will be less successful if we act in obedience to Scripture.

I would take having favor with God over favor with man, but God says you can achieve both. Just make sure you get your priorities right. One is the cause; the other the effect. When we get our priorities right and allow God to take care of the consequences, He will work out all things for our good.

This Scripture tells us that we can be acceptable to men and approved by God. What a powerful way to be effective in the marketplace.

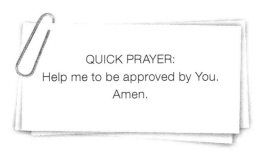

QUICK PRAYER:
Help me to be approved by You.
Amen.

FEBRUARY

18

Rejoice in Your Blessing

"Because the Lord your God will bless you in all your produce and in all the work of your hands, so that you surely rejoice." (Deu 16:15 NKJV)

Enjoy what God has given you. He has blessed you so that you may bless others but also so you will rejoice. Relax and enjoy the blessing of God.

He has said He will bless our produce and the work of our hands. Expect to see His hand at work at your work. Note, however, that we need to work to receive. There is a practical application that is not circumvented by blessing. However, all we have ultimately comes from Him.

If you are not seeing this truth in your life, go to Him and ask why. He will show you the time and season and what you need to do because this is His will, and He is true to His Word.

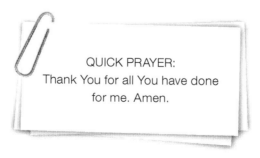

QUICK PRAYER:
Thank You for all You have done
for me. Amen.

Listen!

"Today, if you hear his voice, do not harden your hearts."
(HEB 3:7–8)

God can talk to us in many ways, but it is up to us to choose to listen. First we must shift our hearts and open our minds and spirits to expect to hear from Him.

If you want insight in business, if you want to know what to expect in the future, and if you want to know how to adjust your life to align with the will of God, spend some time with Him. But be willing to change. He will surprise you and soften your heart.

Come to Him in expectation. He is vitally interested in you and your work life. If you haven't experienced this truth, go to Him and ask Him to reveal it to you. You may well get a life-changing revelation.

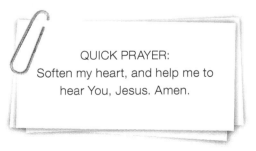

QUICK PRAYER:
Soften my heart, and help me to
hear You, Jesus. Amen.

FEBRUARY

20

God Wants You in Business

"So he called ten of his servants, delivered to them ten minas, and said to them, 'Do business till I come.'" (Luk 19:13 NKJV)

God is intimately interested in your work life. It is not an add-on or just a way to provide. He has asked you to work and will show you how to work in ways you will not expect.

Your ministry and calling is in the marketplace. Expect him to guide and lead you just as a minister in a church will be guided and led. There is no difference in the calling. He wants you in business, where you are most effective.

Oh, and it is okay to relax and enjoy the journey.

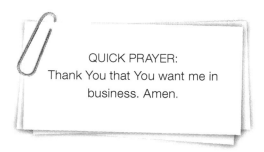

QUICK PRAYER:
Thank You that You want me in
business. Amen.

The Restoration Business

"For the Son of Man came to seek and to save the lost." (LUK 19:10)

What should our priority be? What is our highest imperative? What is God's vision?

Our bottom line is profit or cash flow or a triple bottom-line for some progressive companies. God is vitally interested in bringing success, but He has an ultimate bottom line.

In the midst of your busy life, keep an eye out for an opportunity—a God-given opportunity to share a word, plant a thought, say a prayer, or reap a soul for Jesus. It is the true bottom line and should be our top of mind.

God is in the restoration business, and He will make us all restorers. Jesus came to heal and restore that which was damaged and lost. We are part of His ongoing work.

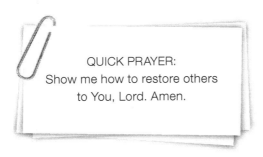

QUICK PRAYER:
Show me how to restore others
to You, Lord. Amen.

FEBRUARY

22

We All Gotta Serve Somebody

"Servants, be submissive to your masters with all fear, not only to the good and gentle, but also to the harsh." (1 Pet 2:18 NKJV)

We all at some time have to report to someone harsh. Maybe it is a shareholder, director, other authority, financier, supplier, or customer. In the midst of our stakeholders and authority figures, there will be some harshness.

So what should be our response? Submission. We should not be a doormat—Jesus was never a doormat—but we must take a submissive stance with a willingness to serve despite how it is received or perceived.

This is a tough call, but this is God's way. He will be with us all the way, equipping us when we have nothing to give.

QUICK PRAYER:
Help me to bear the load when it gets heavy, Lord. Amen.

The Big Picture

"Therefore go and make disciples of all nations..." (MAT 28:19)

This is the ultimate vision and the ultimate goal—pure, simple, and compelling. All our efforts, focus, and resources need to be subjugated to this clarion call.

Alignment to this vision unlocks all the power and resources of God. Why? Because this is His command to us. He came to seek and save the lost. When we disciple, we move a person from hearing the gospel to living a life that demonstrates true transformation. We double our impact as others come to a level of maturity that ensures they are capable of leading and discipling others.

What are we doing to impact our businesses for God? As we influence those around us, we will impact communities, cities, and ultimately nations.

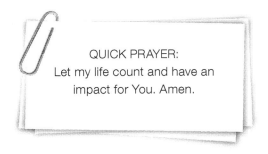

QUICK PRAYER:
Let my life count and have an
impact for You. Amen.

FEBRUARY
24

Want to Lead?

"Give me the wisdom and knowledge to rule them properly, for who could possibly govern this great people of yours?" (2 CHR 1:10 NLT)

If you are a leader, you are going to need some things. How about an increase in wisdom and knowledge? You will find them in God, in His Word, and manifest in His Spirit.

He will equip you for what He has called you to. Anything else would be unreasonable, don't you think? Ask Him for what you need, and watch Him provide.

There is absolutely nothing wrong with leadership aspirations. These desires may well be part of God enabling you to fulfill His purposes in you. However, if you are under the mistaken thought that you can do it without Him, please reconsider.

QUICK PRAYER:
May I have Your wisdom, Lord.
I need it to do what You have
called me to. Amen.

Yes

"But let your 'Yes' be 'Yes,' and your 'No,' 'No'" (Mat 5:37)

There is power in simple truth and when you just walk in simple integrity. One example of this is doing what you say with just a simple yes or a simple no. We often increase complexity in our answers or try to manipulate with a little white lie.

How would others view us if they believed we would always give a straight answer with no hidden agendas, just the truth? When we shared something about God, maybe they would believe that as well. There is something elegant, honest, and pure about simplicity. Keep it simple.

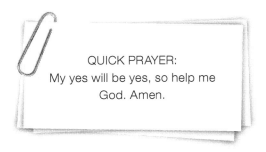

QUICK PRAYER:
My yes will be yes, so help me
God. Amen.

FEBRUARY
26

What Is Stealing?

"You shall not steal" (Exo 20:15)

Let's put aside the obvious stuff. What about downloading illegal music? Taking home stationery? Milking expenses? Or perhaps declaring all taxes due, with no shortcuts? I am surprised how many people don't take their God-given financial and tax obligations seriously.

Then what about time—time with God taken by other things? If we wanted to think a little deeper, we would all be challenged by areas of stealing. Will you take the time to allow God to show you your heart? You may be surprised.

God's measure is absolute. Fortunately, so are His grace, mercy, and forgiveness. Make any corrections you need to make, and move on.

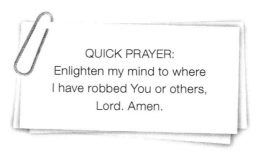

QUICK PRAYER:
Enlighten my mind to where
I have robbed You or others,
Lord. Amen.

God Works

"In the beginning God created..." (GEN 1:1)

How gracious it was of our Creator to model work in His very first act on our behalf. In the beginning He...created—an act of work followed by rest. Is work important to God? Oh yes, it is so important that he acted it out in the very beginning of creation.

Why would He do that unless He wanted to point something out? He values work. Often we work for a wage, a profit, and see it as just a way to provide. God clearly has a different perspective. Will we allow Him to shift our worldview? He took the time to carefully lay out the creative process as a working week. He values our work as a Godly attribute. If it is important to Him, it should be important to us.

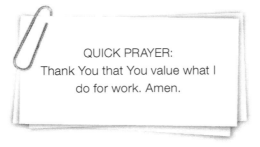

QUICK PRAYER:
Thank You that You value what I do for work. Amen.

FEBRUARY

28

Who Do You Serve?

"Serve wholeheartedly, as if you were serving the Lord, not people." (EPH 6:7)

We will always work for flawed people in a flawed environment. We will be let down, disappointed, not appreciated, and sometimes even taken for granted.

However, if we shift our focus and serve a perfect God, we will look through the imperfect to serve the Perfect. It is all a matter of perspective. The added benefit is we become more effective in the marketplace. We become like that which we focus on. Let's focus on God and shift our mindsets to align with His. This perspective if very powerful and unlocks the service mentality and the ability to see purpose and work wholeheartedly regardless of the circumstances.

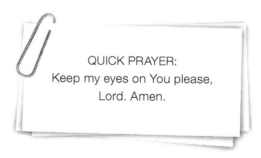

QUICK PRAYER:
Keep my eyes on You please,
Lord. Amen.

Can I Glory in My Work?

"In Christ Jesus, then, I have legitimate reason to glory (exult) in my work for God." (Rom 15:17 AMP)

We work for God. Regardless of our occupation, we are in His employ. Because of this, when we experience success, it is legitimate to glory in it. In fact, we can glory in the very act of service as we work for God in the marketplace.

But what of humility? Surely the ultimate in humility is agreement with God. He says we can glory in our work, so let's drop our false humility and enjoy it as He intended. There is nothing wrong in enjoying all His good gifts. He provides them for our enjoyment and provision and to make us effective in His kingdom.

What a privilege. If we really grasped this truth, it would revolutionize our work life.

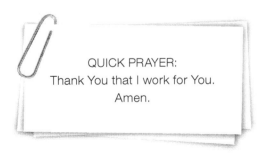

QUICK PRAYER:
Thank You that I work for You.
Amen.

Quick Start?

"So then, just as you received Christ Jesus as Lord, continue to live your lives in him." (Col 2:6)

How good was it when you first gave your life to Jesus? Do you remember that surge of zeal and willingness to tell others of your new experience? What about the sense of release as you left the burden of sin behind?

The Bible implores us not to lose our first love. We need to continue to press into God and deepen that relationship. That takes time. Set aside some time; you may be surprised by what you hear.

It is not a going back but a continuing to press on. Your relationship should always be developing, growing, and changing. If it feels stagnant, begin by seeking to put aside time for Him again.

QUICK PRAYER:
Help me serve You with a pure
heart. Amen.

Payback

"Do not repay evil with evil or insult with insult. On the contrary, repay evil with blessing, because to this you were called so that you may inherit a blessing." (1 Pet 3:9)

Bless those who curse me—are you kidding? Seek out those who hate me and bless them—are you insane? Repaying evil with good seems to not make any sense, but God's ways are not our ways. He has a better view. If we have given our lives to Him, we need to trust Him and do it His way.

We have a choice when our human logic and His Word seem to collide. Often there is an almost paradoxical set of options. He does know better than us, so trust Him to have the answer and follow His ways, and the way becomes clearer.

It is not easy. It is a narrow path, but it is a higher way—a true way.

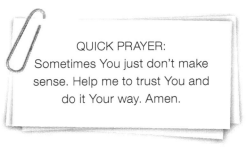

QUICK PRAYER:
Sometimes You just don't make sense. Help me to trust You and do it Your way. Amen.

MARCH
4

Interesting

"Let each of you esteem and look upon and be concerned for not [merely] his own interests, but also each for the interests of others." (Phi 2:4 AMP)

Here is a bombshell: it is not about you. We spend a lot of time with a self-centered view. Take a moment to look to others and see their needs.

Interestingly, we are commanded to esteem, look upon, and be concerned about ourselves and others. This is not a denigration of self but an additional focus on others. So while we are not to undermine ourselves, we do need to raise our awareness of those around us.

As you go about your business today, look around; God may have someone for you to minister to today. In fact, I could almost guarantee it. Often He is just looking for a willing accomplice.

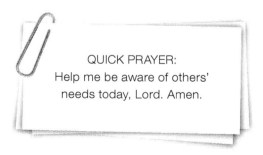

QUICK PRAYER:
Help me be aware of others'
needs today, Lord. Amen.

I Am the Greatest!

"The greatest among you will be your servant." (MAT 23:11)

This truth is perfectly presented in the person of Jesus. The greatest of all was the servant of all. As we seek to serve others, God will exalt us. As we seek to be exulted, He may well oppose the proud. This is counter to human nature because we all want significance and to be esteemed.

There is a part of us that will use others to advance ourselves. We need to be reminded of God's way to counter our own ambition. Let's learn from the Master and learn to serve.

As we choose to be faithful in serving, doors will open that no man can shut, and opportunities will come as we prove to be faithful in the discharge of our God-given responsibilities. Jesus is our example.

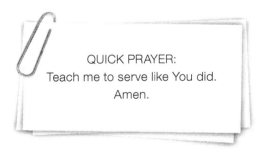

QUICK PRAYER:
Teach me to serve like You did.
Amen.

MARCH

6

God Owns Everything

"To the Lord your God belong the heavens, even the highest heavens, the earth and everything in it." (DEU 10:14)

Everything; now there is an all-encompassing and all-containing word. There are no exceptions, no exclusions, no special cases, and nothing left out. It all belongs to God, whether we agree or not, accept or not, believe or not. If it is in heaven, it is His, and if it is on earth, it is His. All we have and all we think we own are His. If this is true, then we are merely stewards of what belongs to God.

If we really thought about that and understood this fact and all its ramifications, would our lives be different? I think we would be more generous, less frivolous, and more thankful. To begin with, perhaps we should acknowledge that He owns it all, and then maybe He will respond by giving us a greater revelation of how we should steward what is His.

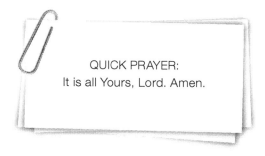

QUICK PRAYER:
It is all Yours, Lord. Amen.

MARCH
7

Abundance

"Lord our God, all this abundance that we have provided for building you a temple for your Holy Name comes from your hand and all of it belongs to you." (1 Chr 29:16)

The promises of God are yes and amen. They are true beyond all doubt. If we are enjoying abundance, it comes from His hand. With abundance comes responsibility. By any worldly standard, we are blessed and have a responsibility of being a part of building the kingdom of God. The nuts and bolts of building and serving in a local church are a part of our responsibility.

Part of our response to receiving from God is an obligation to help sow back into His work. This should come not out of compulsion but out of a grateful heart, thankful in acknowledging that it has all come from Him. He loves to give good gifts to His children, just as we do to ours. He will ensure we are not spoiled, but He is generous.

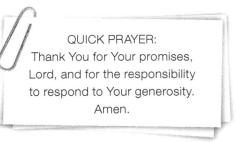

QUICK PRAYER:
Thank You for Your promises,
Lord, and for the responsibility
to respond to Your generosity.
Amen.

MARCH
8

You Can't Argue with God

"Who has a claim against me that I must pay? Everything under heaven belongs to me." (Job 41:11)

Have you ever been in a situation where you are arguing with God? Do you question His will and wisdom? Are you slow to respond to His prompting or argue about the answer to a prayer that may be no when you wanted yes? Perhaps He treats others in a way you want to be treated or you expect Him to do one thing when He does another.

Step back for a moment, and think of just how crazy that is. How asinine; how ridiculous. We are the created; He is the Creator. We have limited vision; He has unlimited knowledge and understanding. Perhaps if we argued less, gave up resisting, and moved quickly to agree and be obedient, we would see much more of the fruit we desire in our lives.

QUICK PRAYER:
Forgive me for arguing and not getting on with doing Your will.
Amen.

Who Does Land Belong To?

"The land must not be sold permanently, because the land is mine and you reside in my land as foreigners and strangers."
(LEV 25:23)

Is God interested in real estate? Yes He is—very interested, as it turns out. A small strip on the edge of the Mediterranean has been the central focus of His redemptive purpose and the attention of the world for generations.

This land, our land, and all land belongs to Him. When we transact or own the land, we are merely leaseholders for our Lord—stewards of His property. Land ownership as we understand it is a misnomer. With this in mind, let us be generous, productive, and mindful when dealing with land and always acknowledge its true owner.

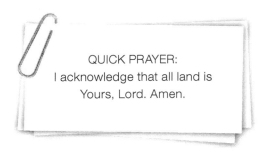

QUICK PRAYER:
I acknowledge that all land is
Yours, Lord. Amen.

MARCH

10

Precious Possessions

"'The silver is mine and the gold is mine,' declares the Lord Almighty." (Hag 2:8)

What do we think about? What occupies our attention? If you are in business, or even if you are not, I am sure material wealth is a core focus for you. We worry about what we have, don't have, want, or feel we need. If we have a lot, we are concerned with its preservation. If we don't have enough, we are concerned about where it will come from. This has two effects: first, it takes our eyes off what is truly important, and second, it causes us concern.

The antidote is a clear understanding of where the true ownership is. If all wealth is God's and we have surrendered to Him and walk in His precepts, He cares for us and will provide all we need. He even promises to give us the desires of our heart. It is all His, truly His, exclusively His. Let's keep our eyes on what is real and eternal, not artificial and temporal.

QUICK PRAYER:
Forgive me for being so focused
on the physical. Amen.

MARCH 11

The Dedication of the Dedicated

"Commit your works to the Lord and your plans will be established." (Pro 16:3 NASB)

When you are making plans, please be careful. Invite God into what you are doing. He may well have a different agenda. Prayerfully consider any important decision, and seek the wise counsel of others.

Make a point of committing your works to God. Offer them up to Him in a specific way that you are comfortable with. Doing this will allow His blessing to fall and His wisdom to prevail. You will see opportunities you didn't see before and be amazed at the way things begin to line up.

When times are tough, you will know God is with you as you have committed your business to Him.

> QUICK PRAYER:
> Father, I once again commit my business to You. Lead me, guide me, and establish my plans according to Your will and Word.

Do You Listen—I Mean Really Listen?

"Without consultation, plans are frustrated, but with many counselors they succeed." (Pro 15:22 NASB)

When we are in leadership, we often feel we need to be seen to have all the answers. Often we think we do have all the answers. The Scriptures are very clear that, despite our blind confidence, we don't. We need others' perspectives to get a holistic view.

Often in our business we are removed from the reality of day-to-day contact with customers and suppliers. Those on the front line will often have massive insights into our problems and opportunities.

Even when identified, open dialogue and input are desirable for a clear view. Proverbs 19:20 emphasizes the point, saying, *"Listen to counsel and accept discipline, that you may be wise the rest of your days"* (NASB).

QUICK PRAYER:
Lord, help me to listen to those
You have placed around me.
Amen.

MARCH 13

Do You Have a Plan?

"The plans of the diligent lead surely to advantage, but everyone who is hasty comes surely to poverty." (PRO 21:5 NASB)

The old adage goes, "If you fail to plan, you plan to fail." Is it a cliché, yes, but it is nonetheless true, and the Scriptures agree. I have seen many business plans that have been so long and so complex that they are rendered useless. They go straight in someone's bottom drawer, only to see the light of day at the next 'strategic review.'

Planning in its purest sense is clearly identifying what you want to look like in the future. Take a view—say three years hence—and very clearly, and more importantly, demonstrably and empirically, write down in the simplest measurable terms what your business should look like. Then work out the simple steps to get there, and ensure your people are empowered to deliver their piece.

QUICK PRAYER:
Lord, help me to plan, and as I commit these plans to You, bring them to pass according to Your Word. Thank You and amen.

MARCH
14

Our God Is the God of the Breakthrough.

"Surely there is a future and your hope will not be cut off."
(Pro 23:18 NASB)

Sometimes life is tough—often very tough. But we serve a God who is a Redeemer.

Regardless of what you face today, there is hope in God. Even self-inflicted trouble can be redeemed by Him. King David, the adulterer and murderer who took another man's wife and had her husband killed, was forgiven and his situation redeemed. The fruit of this relationship was Solomon, the greatest and wisest of all men. God created a future and hope and was David's salvation.

There is a future, and God loves you, cares about you, and died for you. He still has a plan and purpose for your life, regardless of your circumstances.

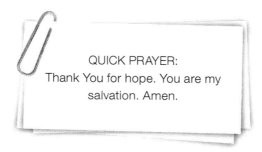

QUICK PRAYER:
Thank You for hope. You are my salvation. Amen.

Do You Know the Way Forward?

"There is a way that seems right to a man, but in the end it leads to death." (Pro 14:12 NIV1984)

Sometimes our natural tendencies can come to the fore. Pausing to seek God's wisdom can often shift our view and may save us from an unseen consequence. It is worth considering that we are not always right and that God has a better view.

When we belong to God, we are in His kingdom, under His jurisdiction. To prosper in this realm, we need to follow the auspices of the King. Doing it God's way should be our prime modus operandi, even when it doesn't make worldly sense. But occasionally we need some specific insight. Asking God and expecting an answer is part and parcel of a walk with a personal Savior.

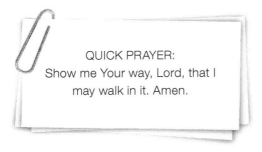

QUICK PRAYER:
Show me Your way, Lord, that I
may walk in it. Amen.

MARCH

How Do We Align Our Thoughts to God's Will?

"Roll your works upon the Lord [commit and trust them wholly to Him; He will cause your thoughts to become agreeable to His will, and] so shall your plans be established and succeed." (PRO 16:3 AMP)

If only my thoughts were aligned to God's will. Take a look at this Scripture. If we cast our works onto Him, commit and trust them to Him, He will make us think along the lines of His will. Why? So our plans will work and we will have success!

That is staggering in its significance. If we trust Him, He will turn our hearts to His will. We know that if we are in His will, He will guide us and lead us. How comforting it is to know that as we commit our works to Him, He will turn us to not only hear from Him, but our very thoughts will become His thoughts. Then we truly will have the mind of Christ.

QUICK PRAYER:
I commit my business to You.
Please align my thoughts to Your
will, that my plans may succeed.
Amen.

MARCH 17

Need Some Insight?

"And if you call out for insight and cry aloud for understanding, and if you look for it as for silver and search for it as for hidden treasure, then you will understand the fear of the Lord and find the knowledge of God." (Pro 2:3–5 NIV1984)

Imagine the smartest guys in the world all in the same room—the business world's who's who. Buffet, Jobs, Gates, Morgan, whoever you want. You have absolute access. How exciting would that be?

We have access to a mind, an understanding, a power of change, and a foreseer of all with an infinite capacity and all the time and individual attention we want. Yet sometimes we lose the comprehension of such access. It cost a lot—more than money can buy. Let's not take it for granted.

There is an essence in the Scripture that understanding and wisdom need to be toiled for, as searching for gold or silver. There is a measure of discipline, sweat, dedication, and work required. Will we pay the price for insight beyond our realm of understanding? Will we seek the wisdom of God? Wow, what a privilege to have access to the throne room of unfathomable grace.

QUICK PRAYER:
Please give me insight into those things that prevail against me.
Amen.

MARCH
18

How Straight Is Your Path?

"In all your ways acknowledge him, and he will make your paths straight." (PRO 3:6 NIV1984)

How many times has God helped you out? How many times has He provided for you in your hour of need? Many times He works for our advantage and we are completely unaware of it.

So what should our response be? How often do we acknowledge Him in what we do, what we say, and how we act? We can acknowledge it to Him. Saying thank you to God is an important part of prayer.

"Doing life" His way is a major way of acknowledging His lordship in our lives. Acknowledging His lordship in our influence and success, or overcoming life's problems, is not only a witness but also will help align ourselves to His will. When all is said and done and we stand before God, the complexity of our journey will be shown to have been a straight path, where we have acknowledged Him and done it His way.

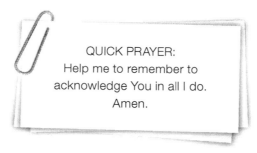

QUICK PRAYER:
Help me to remember to
acknowledge You in all I do.
Amen.

A Kingdom Law

"One man gives freely, yet gains even more; another withholds unduly, but comes to poverty." (Pro 11:24 NIV1984)

In the world, we are taught that if we are tight with our money, we will get more, yet the law of the kingdom is the opposite. Give and it will be given unto you. Withhold and you will come to poverty. It sounds upside down, but how often is that true with the things that God asks of us? He had to die to bring life. Death led to victory.

There is very often joy in obedience. As we give, it changes our hearts. Have you met a happy person who is stingy or a very generous person who is not happy? The Bible also tells us that it is God who gives us the gift of enjoying wealth. I think this comes from having a generous heart.

QUICK PRAYER:
Holy Spirit, please cause me to have a generous heart, a fruit of Your presence in me. Amen.

MARCH
20

Eaten Your Words Recently?

"The tongue has the power of life and death, and those who love it will eat its fruit." (Pro 18:21)

You are what you say. God spoke the world into being, and we are created in His image. How many have been damaged by having negative words spoken over them by a parent, teacher, or minister?

Describing the tongue as having the power of life and death is about as strong a term as you could use. God is obviously placing a massive emphasis on the importance of what we say, so therefore, should we. Watch what you say, be measured in your words, and encourage, build up, and edify those around you and yourself. You will inhabit the world created by your words.

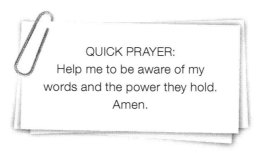

QUICK PRAYER:
Help me to be aware of my
words and the power they hold.
Amen.

What Comes First?

"Honor the Lord with your wealth, with the firstfruits of all your crops." (Pro 3:9)

The principle of giving a portion is infused in the Scriptures. Honoring God with a holy portion, tithe, or sacrifice is a spiritual principle. If it is all His, why not honor Him with acknowledging His Lordship by bringing the tithe into the storehouse?

This is not a legalistic practice but a Godly discipline and acknowledgment that all we have comes from Him. It helps keep it all in perspective. We think so much about these things that a fresh perspective is probably not a bad thing.

He doesn't need your money, but He does require your obedience. I have found that a surrendered heart moderates greed. Perhaps we need to give to receive.

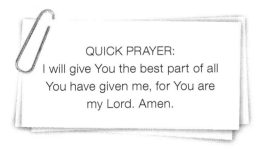

QUICK PRAYER:
I will give You the best part of all You have given me, for You are my Lord. Amen.

MARCH

22

A Promise

"Honor the Lord with your wealth, with the firstfruits of all your crops; then your barns will be filled to overflowing, and your vats will brim over with new wine." (Pro 3:9–10)

Wow! What a promise. All the promises of God are "yes and amen" to those who love Jesus (see 2 Cor 1:20). You will have more than enough when you are faithful and honor God with your income. His Word is true; He is not a man that He would lie (see Num 23:19). Do we dare to accept Him according to His Word and exercise faith and action to appropriate His promise?

This is a mind-bending promise but one that is true because God said it was so. How we honor God with our first fruits is between us and God, and many errors have been placed on this truth. The important part is recognizing the truth of His provision and actually acting on it to reflect the command to honor Him with the cream of the crop.

QUICK PRAYER:
Thank You that you are a generous God. Please bless me according to Your Word, as I have sought to be faithful to Your will. Amen.

You Don't Make Sense, God

"Trust in the Lord with all your heart and lean not on your own understanding." (PRO 3:5)

How often do we take circumstances and try to figure out the meaning. We look at our business or things that happen and can't make sense of them.

An infinite God has a different perspective. How do we ever expect to understand him? We won't. His ways are not our ways, his thoughts not our thoughts. Sometimes we need to understand that we won't understand and just...trust.

Often just as we think we have God in a box, and understand Him, things change and the mystery continues. It is just a part of our walk with God. Why don't we just let God be God, we don't always have to understand.

QUICK PRAYER:
I will trust You. Amen.

MARCH

24

How Do I Get Knowledge?

"The fear of the Lord is the beginning of knowledge, but fools despise wisdom and instruction." (Pro 1:7)

What is knowledge? Is it just the accumulation of facts or something deeper? In my view, it needs to be applicable to have any value. The fear of God is described as the beginning of knowledge, the foundation of understanding. This is not just some ethereal understanding of God but a practical knowledge that is applicable in the real world, in our everyday existence at work.

If wisdom is to develop, we need to know that God is God and that His Word is revelation. If you want knowledge, go to God, read His Word, and ask His Spirit to reveal its treasures to you. Do this and you will have knowledge, instruction, and wisdom.

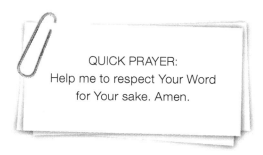

QUICK PRAYER:
Help me to respect Your Word
for Your sake. Amen.

Protect Yourself

"Above all else, guard your heart, for everything you do flows from it." (Pro 4:23)

Our hearts are hard to understand. They are the wellspring of emotion, feelings, motivators, and passions. We can damage our hearts by exposing them to the wrong influences, and they can be deceptive.

This Scripture tells us that everything we do flows from our hearts. Wow, now that is something we just do not understand. Even what we say is influenced as "out of our hearts our mouths speak" (Mat 12:34). Be careful of potentially destructive relationships in your business and private world, and do your utmost to protect your heart. It is obviously an important part to protect.

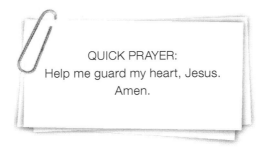

QUICK PRAYER:
Help me guard my heart, Jesus.
Amen.

Need a Shield?

"Every word of God is flawless; he is a shield to those who take refuge in him." (Pro 30:5)

We all need protection. From time to time we are attacked. We are in a war; we should expect some flak. So how do we defend ourselves and fight back? Jesus used the Word of God as a weapon.

In this Scripture, we are advised to use God's Word as a shield. If you find yourself in trouble in business or in your personal life, speak the Word of God. Get to know your armory. You never know when you will need it. If you take the time to study the Bible, it will become a part of who you are. Speaking the Word was modeled to us by Jesus. How much more we need that protection!

QUICK PRAYER:
Protect me when I need a shield,
Lord. Teach me to use Your
Word. Amen.

MARCH
27

Who Keeps You Sharp?

"As iron sharpens iron, so one person sharpens another."
(PRO 27:17)

Who keeps you sharp? Who do you have in your life who you trust—who you can "do life with"? We all need people who love God who can keep us sharp.

Often in our busy lives those relationships have drifted away or may not even exist. Ask God today to bring someone into your life or reacquaint yourself with a true friend. Why not schedule in some time to stay sharp with good company?

Be careful of a life with many acquaintances and no true friends. We all need some accountability. In order to gain true friendship, we need to be a true friend. As in any relationship, we will only get out what we put in. Investing in friendship is a sure way to surround yourself with great friends.

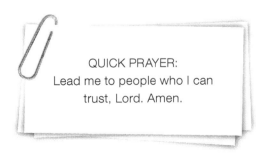

QUICK PRAYER:
Lead me to people who I can
trust, Lord. Amen.

MARCH
28

Instructions

"Where there is no revelation, people cast off restraint; but blessed is the one who heeds wisdom's instruction." (Pro 29:18)

What is revelation? It is an insight from God. Wow! Imagine having access to someone who knows everything, sees everything, knows everyone, and can see into the future.

We absolutely have that with God, yet we tend to take it for granted. If you need some direction in your business, He is vitality interested in your work life. Imagine the opportunity to talk with the ultimate business guru. Would you go out of your way for an hour with Jobs or Gates? Well, you have access to someone far, far superior, better connected, and infinitely more capable. Why not spend some time with Him and get your revelation?

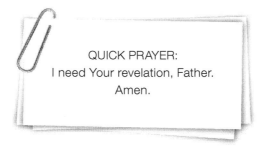

QUICK PRAYER:
I need Your revelation, Father.
Amen.

Three Things

"For receiving instruction in prudent behavior, doing what is right and just and fair." (Pro 1:3)

Here is a quick checklist that should guide all our behavior in business: Is it right? Is it just? Is it fair? Often these are not considered in a business context, but if we are endeavoring to do it God's way, then this should be our context.

We get these instructions from revelation through the Word of God. Sometimes our view of what is just and fair may not be God's view. But His perspective will help us be prudent and do what is right. How would you like people to describe you? Right, just, and fair would be a good start.

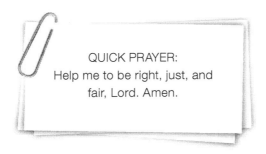

QUICK PRAYER:
Help me to be right, just, and fair, Lord. Amen.

MARCH
30

Need More Understanding?

"The fear of the Lord is the beginning of wisdom, and knowledge of the Holy One is understanding." (PRO 9:10)

I don't know about you, but I could do with more understanding—in particular an understanding that comes from the revelation of listening to the Holy Spirit. He is waiting to be invited into your business and wants to walk with you, guiding, leading, empowering, and bringing understanding.

Let's not relegate God's wisdom and our understanding to a seemingly sacred context. Being vitally interested in our vocation, our calling at work, He is always willing to give insight. Invite Him into your business world again today.

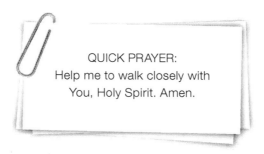

QUICK PRAYER:
Help me to walk closely with
You, Holy Spirit. Amen.

God Is in Control

"In their hearts humans plan their course, but the Lord establishes their steps." (PRO 16:9)

If we have given our lives to God, He will guide our paths. What a reassurance that He is indeed in control. So should we stop planning? No, of course not. But in our planning, let's invite God to participate. He will anyway, so why not get an inside view? It can often be an easier journey.

We will plan and push out in a direction, but it is God who will establish our steps, God who will watch over the direction, and ultimately He who will determine the way. I take a lot of comfort in that.

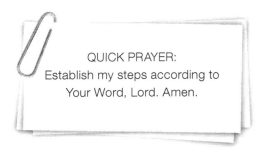

QUICK PRAYER:
Establish my steps according to
Your Word, Lord. Amen.

APRIL
1

I'm Not Proud

"Pride goes before destruction, a haughty spirit before a fall."
(PRO 16:18)

Ouch. With a Scripture like that, it behooves us to remain humble. Humility is not a "I'm just a worm" view; it is a perspective that agrees with God and a focus that doesn't exult ourselves at the expense of others.

It is a position that acknowledges that all we have and all we are comes from God. He is the author and perfector of our faith; all good things come from Him. To think that we are somehow responsible for the gifts we have or the influence we have is not only proud; it is also naive.

QUICK PRAYER:
Forgive me for my self-reliance. I
put my trust in You, Lord. Amen.

APRIL
2

Be Gentle

"A gentle answer turns away wrath, but a harsh word stirs up anger." (PRO 15:1)

When we are in a position of authority in our company, there is a temptation to be harsh. We can easily display emotions that are not appropriate. This is especially true when we are faced with an angry person.

The wisdom of this Scripture is that an unexpectedly gentle response can disarm a potentially volatile situation. Often when we are challenged, we may assume a gentle answer is a sign of weakness and that authority demands a certain demeanor. This Scripture would indicate a better way.

Leadership does not demand that we act in a harsh or distant manner. Our example is Jesus. How did He act? Take a look in the gospels for an example of true leadership in action.

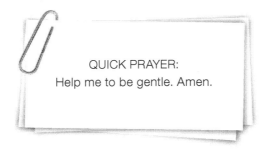

QUICK PRAYER:
Help me to be gentle. Amen.

APRIL

3

Need a Straight Path?

"In all your ways submit to him, and he will make your paths straight." (Pro 3:6)

What a great promise—a straight path, true, accurate, full of purpose and direction, with a sense of accomplishment. The required condition is surrender. Giving it all to God is a constant state, not a onetime event. We often see submission in a negative context, but here we learn that its outcome is positive and beneficial.

This is particularly true in business, where we are making decisions constantly and busy in a rapidly changing environment. Pause, take a moment, and submit your situation to God. You will be surprised by how straight that path can be.

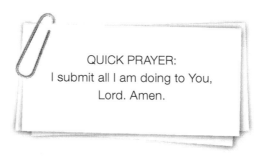

QUICK PRAYER:
I submit all I am doing to You,
Lord. Amen.

Friends

"One who has unreliable friends soon comes to ruin, but there is a friend who sticks closer than a brother." (Pro 18:24)

Businesspeople tend to have a lot of acquaintances but not too many friends. Taking the time to build deeper friendships is a great investment. Character-full friends who will be with you regardless of circumstances have enormous value. Perhaps you too can be a friend like that and enrich someone else's life.

We are all busy, but when we take the time to invest in others, we find ourselves surrounded by friends. The ones who give and take, who love with reciprocity, who live transparently, and who will hold us in mutual accountability—those are our true friends.

Like all worthwhile things, true friendships develop over time, need care and consideration, and can endure the good times and the bad.

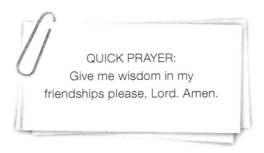

QUICK PRAYER:
Give me wisdom in my
friendships please, Lord. Amen.

APRIL

5

Ants!

"Go to the ant, you sluggard; consider its ways and be wise!"
(PRO 6:6)

I don't like ants, but they have enormous energy and strength. They never seem to rest. They are always productive and busy. There is a lesson of a need for application and hard work.

There is fruit from good, honest labor, focus, and application. If we wait for it to happen by itself, it probably won't. We have a responsibility to be productive with the gifts and resources given to us. In a very real way, we are, and will be, held accountable.

Take a moment to reflect on your application. Are you focused and applying your resources with wisdom?

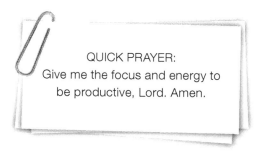

QUICK PRAYER:
Give me the focus and energy to
be productive, Lord. Amen.

Tongue Holding

"Whoever derides their neighbor has no sense, but the one who has understanding holds their tongue." (PRO 11:12)

Sometimes the best thing you can say is nothing at all. Giving someone a piece of your mind may be a piece you can ill afford to lose.

There is grace in overlooking an offense, mercy in not taking retribution, and forgiveness in answering gently to a harsh critic. Grace, mercy, and forgiveness are all things that have been freely given to us.

Let's treat others as God has treated us. Thank goodness He does not give us what we deserve. Why not treat others as God treats us? Our businesses will be all the better for it.

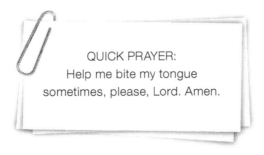

QUICK PRAYER:
Help me bite my tongue
sometimes, please, Lord. Amen.

APRIL

7

A Change of Heart

"In the Lord's hand the king's heart is a stream of water that he channels toward all who please him." (PRO 21:1)

God has the power to change a man's heart. He has the influence to give you favor amongst men and a willingness to open doors for His children. As His follower, you have a right to ask for His influence and favor. He may say no, or he may open a door that seems stuck fast.

Why not ask and see him empower you and your business as you seek to serve Him? The right favor and the right time can bring breakthrough change. Sometimes we look at an option and say, "That would never happen." But God is the God of the breakthrough, quite capable of moving a man's heart and giving you favor. Ask Him; you may be surprised at the outcome.

QUICK PRAYER:
Lord, would you incline the heart
of those in authority toward me,
please? Amen.

APRIL
8

Have Enough?

"Better a little with the fear of the Lord than great wealth with turmoil." (Pro 15:16)

How much is really enough? What price are you paying for the extra you think you need? Is the ambition to be wealthier fogging your focus on God? That is a key question. Please think about that for a moment. Don't dismiss it out of hand; it may apply to you.

Sometimes the price you pay is too much for the prize. What price are you paying? What price is your family paying?

Being grateful for what we already have can disempower the greed and consumerism that so easily ensnare us. Being content is a Godly attribute and reflects true priorities and a recognition that He has our best in mind.

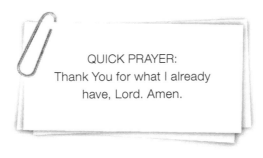

QUICK PRAYER:
Thank You for what I already
have, Lord. Amen.

APRIL

9

A Good Name

"A good name is more desirable than great riches; to be esteemed is better than silver or gold." (Pro 22:1)

Avoiding shortcuts and not burning bridges are two ways of protecting your reputation. Being pleasant to deal with, regardless of how difficult a situation or how bad a deal goes, will ensure your reputation stays in place.

The Bible places such things above material gain and above precious jewels. We too should have the same perspective. We are the physical manifestation of God's love to the world, after all. Often people will judge God by how they see us.

Protecting our reputation protects God's reputation; we are, after all, His representatives.

QUICK PRAYER:
Please protect my reputation.
Amen.

Am I a Fountain?

"The mouth of the righteous is a fountain of life, but the mouth of the wicked conceals violence." (Pro 10:11)

Fountains are wonderful. They are refreshing, life giving, beautiful, and awe inspiring. Our words should refresh, encourage, and inspire those around us.

The alternative doesn't bear too much consideration. Today be aware of what you say. Are you speaking life or death? Your mouth should be a fountain of life.

Try and be conscious of what you say and its possible impact. If you are anything like me, you will be surprised by how little you say that enlightens the life of others. Maybe that is why the wise seem to speak little and listen a lot.

Look for the opportunity to refresh someone at work this week. You well may be surprised by the reaction, though I would hope it is not one of total surprise.

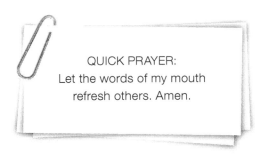

QUICK PRAYER:
Let the words of my mouth
refresh others. Amen.

APRIL

11

Correction

"Whoever loves discipline loves knowledge, but whoever hates correction is stupid." (Pro 12:1)

It is easy to forget that God is our Father, and like all good fathers, He will bring correction and discipline from time to time. This is often manifested in difficult circumstances or a word from someone else. How should we react to these events?

Getting before God to understand what adjustments He wants to make in us is a good start. We can be thankful that we have a loving Father who wants the best for us. Our position in receiving discipline and correction will determine our ultimate altitude in life and our walk with Him.

If you keep getting a "Why am I here again?" feeling, you may not have learned the lesson yet.

QUICK PRAYER:
I need Your correction in my life, Lord. Help me to be aware.
Amen.

Big Mouth

"Speak up for those who cannot speak for themselves, for the rights of all who are destitute." (Pro 31:8)

If you are in a leadership position in business, God has given you influence. What will you use it for? To bless yourself and your family? Yes, that is fine. To bless others in your company or church? That is fine too. But what of those who have no voice in society, those who have no influence or resources—who will speak for them? How will their voice be heard and justice done?

Often we see life through our own worldview, blissfully unaware of others who are less fortunate than ourselves. It is our duty to look again and ask how we can help. You can make a difference. Is God speaking to you today?

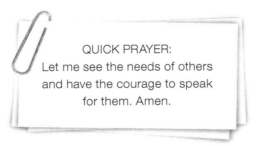

QUICK PRAYER:
Let me see the needs of others
and have the courage to speak
for them. Amen.

APRIL

13

Need Direction

"She gives no thought to the way of life; her paths wander aimlessly, but she does not know it." (Pro 5:6)

Where are you going? What are you trying to achieve? What is the future state of your company that you are aiming to get to? We all need direction in order to focus, to allocate resources, and to create vision and momentum. If we don't know where we are going, how will we know when we get there?

Don't be aimless and wander. Ask God for clarity of direction. He has a plan and purpose for your life. Part of our destiny is orchestrated and for part we need to partner with God, hear from Him, and impact our circumstances with faith prayer and action.

How can we be obedient if we do not hear, and how can we hear if we do not listen?

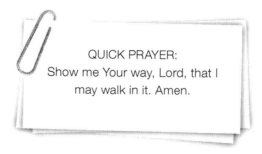

QUICK PRAYER:
Show me Your way, Lord, that I
may walk in it. Amen.

A Time of Plenty

"Yet it stores its provisions in summer and gathers its food at harvest." (Pro 6:8)

Life comes in seasons. There is a time to plant, a time to wait, a time to harvest, and a time to store away grain. How we act and what we do with our resources should be driven by an awareness of what season we are in. Economies have seasons, as do businesses.

Do not assume plenty will always be there. Alternatively, if you see no fruit but have sown faithfully, your harvest will be coming. Sometimes it rains in summer and the sun shines in winter. Discerning timing is a key part of a successful business. God can give you that insight.

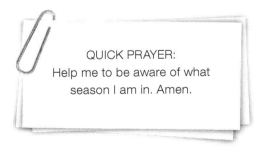

QUICK PRAYER:
Help me to be aware of what
season I am in. Amen.

APRIL

15

Evil Talkers

"Evildoers are trapped by their sinful talk, and so the innocent escape trouble." (PRO 12:13)

Talk, talk, talk. We do a lot of it, in particular in leadership positions. But how much is really constructive? We also talk a lot of rubbish sometimes, or is that just me? If evildoers are trapped in their talk, we should be aware of this lesson and ensure our talk is liberating, encouraging, and limited.

This word also seems to show a path of escape as others trap themselves in their talk. Wisdom would therefore commend some careful consideration before talking. Sometimes saying nothing is an appropriate response. We can be profound just in our silence, and there is a time to say nothing and to walk away.

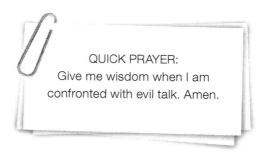

QUICK PRAYER:
Give me wisdom when I am
confronted with evil talk. Amen.

APRIL
16

Targeted Marketing

"How useless to spread a net where every bird can see it!"
(PRO 1:17)

We live in a world that is saturated with overt marketing and an information highway driven by social media. Blatant marketing is now receiving the disdain of educated and critical consumers. We need to be much smarter in how we present our products in a desirable light.

Influencing the influencers, experiential marketing, social responsibility, and alignment with good causes are all good ways to target marketing without shouting about the brand and getting a negative response.

If you want to be really creative, how about asking the Creator? In Him are the fullness of creativity and the fullness of wisdom. What an indescribable resource.

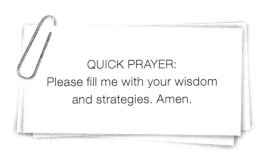

QUICK PRAYER:
Please fill me with your wisdom
and strategies. Amen.

APRIL

17

Rebuke

"Repent at my rebuke! Then I will pour out my thoughts to you, I will make known to you my teachings." (Pro 1:23)

I hate discipline. When God is working on something in my life, those adjustments are sometimes not easy. However, as we respond to those things, God begins to talk to us, reveal more of Himself, and make known more of His character and ways. Sometimes we miss out on His blessings because we resist His correction.

These corrections are always for a purpose. He will often highlight a behavior because it may well cause us to stumble down the track. He doesn't do it for His entertainment but for our greater good.

His promise is to "pour out His thoughts." Imagine that—thinking the thoughts of God.

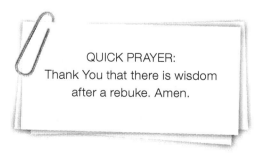

QUICK PRAYER:
Thank You that there is wisdom
after a rebuke. Amen.

APRIL
18

Wisdom

"Do not forsake wisdom, and she will protect you; love her, and she will watch over you." (Pro 4:6)

There are two kinds of wisdom: worldly wisdom and Godly wisdom. The worldly kind is fine, but in Godly wisdom we gain an eternal perspective and the wisdom of ages—the wisdom of a Creator who knows us intimately and formed us individually.

Pressing into God and seeking His wisdom has great benefit in all we do as we serve God in the marketplace. Godly wisdom is often in contrast to worldly wisdom, and the truly wise can discern the difference.

True wisdom always originates with Him Who is wisdom. He is not only the origin of all true wisdom; He is wisdom itself. Wisdom is a characteristic of who God is. When you seek wisdom, you are seeking Him.

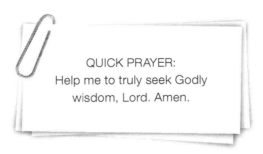

QUICK PRAYER:
Help me to truly seek Godly
wisdom, Lord. Amen.

APRIL

19

Do It Right

"Such are the paths of all who go after ill-gotten gain; it takes away the life of those who get it." (Pro 1:19)

There is a big price to pay for doing things the wrong way. Often it looks like an easy answer; a quick win, cut a few corners, no one will know. But God knows and sees and is concerned.

In business we face many choices of integrity every day. Let's commit to doing it God's way and let Him sort out the consequences. Let's do it right and honor Him.

There is a price to pay for doing it the wrong way and a reward to reap for doing it right. You will know in your heart what is right and what is wrong. His law is now written on your heart, and when we incline our ear to our hearts, we will know what is right.

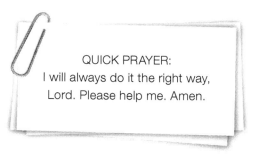

QUICK PRAYER:
I will always do it the right way,
Lord. Please help me. Amen.

Sshhhh, It's a Secret

"Gossips betray a confidence, but a trustworthy person keeps a secret." (PRO 11:13)

Gossip is described in Scripture as a "choice morsel," and often it is. Perhaps it is a juicy bit of gossip only a few know. Or maybe we have been entrusted with a secret, a confidence has been entrusted to us. How do we respond?

This is an important question because our ability to keep a secret speaks to our character. Being a person of integrity with an ability to be trusted makes us a safe place. When we are trusted, what we say is listened to. It takes a lot to build trust and only a single event to destroy it.

Our reputations are intrinsically intertwined with the reputation of Him Whom we serve. When we let ourselves down, we tarnish God's reputation because we declare Him as our Lord.

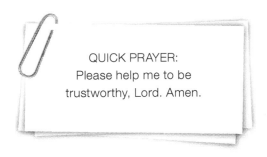

QUICK PRAYER:
Please help me to be
trustworthy, Lord. Amen.

APRIL

21

Lip Fruit

"From the fruit of their lips people are filled with good things, and the work of their hands brings them reward." (Pro 12:14)

Do you want to be filled with good things? Speak well and work hard. These two things go hand in hand. Individually they have an effect and together they produce good fruit. God says that as you operate in this way, you will be filled with good things and rewarded.

In business and our personal lives, we impact people. What we say has the power to build up or tear down. That influence on people often determines our success in all realms of life.

We can say good things and do good things. Both are important and part of our witness at work.

QUICK PRAYER:
Thank You that You value good
words and good work. Amen.

Overcoming Big Problems

"One who is wise can go up against the city of the mighty and pull down the stronghold in which they trust." (Pro 21:22)

Every so often we face big problems. These are not the ordinary things of life but those massive, almost overwhelming problems that rarely impact us but that can be very intimidating. This is when we really need the wisdom of God. Let Him lay down the strategy, and in His strength you can overcome and pull down the mighty stronghold.

Take the time to wait on Him for an answer. Often a big problem causes an immediate response from us. We want to act because we feel doing nothing is ignoring the problem. Taking time to hear from God can result in a suitable response empowered by the God Who overcomes.

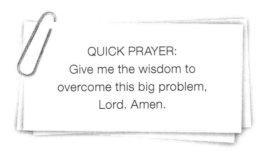

QUICK PRAYER:
Give me the wisdom to
overcome this big problem,
Lord. Amen.

APRIL

23

Love

"Better a small serving of vegetables with love than a fattened calf with hatred." (PRO 15:17)

Love is not a word we often use in a business context. Here we are talking about the price we sometimes pay to live a life with a few extras. Getting a balance in life where we know our priorities and see our responsibilities clearly can have a great impact.

We have a need to be loved and to love. Don't let your work under the disguise of providing, destroy the very people you love. We are called to provide, and that goes well beyond the financials. We have responsibilities for ourselves, our immediate families, those around us, and the greater kingdom of God.

We need to look at our relationships for a holistic perspective in order to judge reasonably.

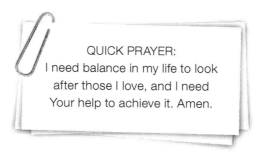

QUICK PRAYER:
I need balance in my life to look after those I love, and I need Your help to achieve it. Amen.

Chance

"The lot is cast into the lap, but its every decision is from the Lord." (PRO 16:33)

When is chance just chance? Is fate really fate? Our self-centered nature demands a sense of self-reliance, where we can dictate our terms and influence and control our futures. The idea that there is a random universe that God asserts His influence over occasionally has an innate appeal.

But the bad news, or should I say good news, is that God is in control—so much so that even when lots are cast, something we consider pure chance, He dictates the outcome. Just to emphasize the point, the Scripture tells us "its every decision" comes from Him. We might prefer an occasionally rather than an every, but get used to it—He is in control.

QUICK PRAYER:
Thank You that what happens to me is not random but has purpose. Amen.

APRIL

25

Revelation

"He reveals deep and hidden things; he knows what lies in darkness, and light dwells with him." (Dan 2:22)

Daniel knew God. These powerhouse biblical figures have taken on the persona of legends, but they were flesh and blood like us. They sinned like we do, failed like we do, and had the concerns and worries of life just as we experience. If they were like us, we can like them.

Daniel knew how to pray. He was disciplined to setting aside time to converse with God. He knew God just as we can know God. His time with God was a dialogue with the Creator, not a list of his needs. Daniel tells us here that God reveals deep and hidden things, knows what we can't see, and can warn and show us these things. If you want insight into opportunity for your business, you will need to walk with God closer. Insight, wisdom, and instruction are accompanied by peace, joy, and the occasional correction. Listen and learn.

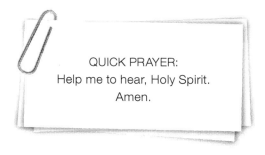

QUICK PRAYER:
Help me to hear, Holy Spirit.
Amen.

APRIL
26

Trouble Maker

"All his brothers and sisters and everyone who had known him before came and ate with him in his house. They comforted and consoled him over all the trouble the Lord had brought on him, and each one gave him a piece of silver and a gold ring." (JOB 42:11)

What! God causing trouble? I am not sure that fits in with my "come-to-Jesus-and-everything-will-be-okay" theology. Unfortunately God is bigger than our image of Him or our attempts to put Him in a box. We may have experienced and adopted the milk of the word; well, this one is more like the broccoli—probably good for you but not a great experience.

The Lord will allow all sorts of things to befall us. We need to understand the difference between what needs to be submitted to and endured, what needs our persistence to overcome, and that which is an attack to repel. To get that level of understanding, we need an ongoing relationship with God to lead and guide us. If the experience of trouble has been sanctioned from heaven, learn well and surrender fast. It's a much easier journey.

QUICK PRAYER:
If it is You Who has allowed this trouble, help me to endure and learn well. Amen.

APRIL

27

Calamities

"Is it not from the mouth of the Most High that both calamities and good things come?" (LAM 3:38)

Hard times from God; I am not sure I want to hear that. Surely a loving Father would not allow such things to happen. Yet His ways are not our ways. His thoughts are not our thoughts. He has eternal things in mind while we focus on the temporal.

Our surrender to God is not only an invitation for Him to come in but a willingness to let Him be Lord, here and now, in the good and the bad. But let us not forget the life after this one—a future with Him, a heaven to gain and a hell to avoid. His free gift is eternal life, but it cost Him His Son. His love for us in intimate and infinite; it is in the hard times that we truly learn to trust.

QUICK PRAYER:
Thank You for the good and
hard times that can come from
Your hand, Lord. Amen.

Favor

"The Lord was with him; he showed him kindness and granted him favor in the eyes of the prison warden." (GEN 39:21)

The Lord showed him kindness and favor. Which of us would not want more of that? We who are called to His purposes and surrendered to His will are able to solicit His favor. That can be manifest in many ways. Resistance can fall away, the hearts of those who oppose us can shift, and we can expect favor from those in authority over us.

There is something about walking closely with God that creates an atmosphere. This can shift mindsets and circumstances. Sometimes just our presence in a place or situation can move opposition or bring resolution. This is no source of pride because it is not us; it is the Holy Spirit Who indwells us, and His anointing can literally move mountains.

Be bold. Why not seek His will and ask for His favor? You may be surprised by just how willing He is to move on your behalf to accomplish His will.

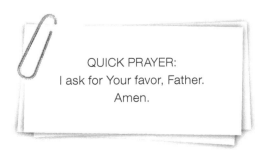

QUICK PRAYER:
I ask for Your favor, Father.
Amen.

A Change of Heart

"'And may I have a letter to Asaph, keeper of the royal park, so he will give me timber to make beams for the gates of the citadel by the temple and for the city wall and for the residence I will occupy?' And because the gracious hand of my God was on me, the king granted my requests." (Neh 2:8)

I like this Scripture because it says two things. Here was an audacious request for resources, but the answer was due to the gracious hand of God. This is the essence of what it is to walk with God in the marketplace—hearing from God, moving with passion and big goals, asking for favor, and seeing the hand of God move and work miracles in provision and outcomes.

Nehemiah was under no illusion about who is accomplishing the task and gave due credit to His Lord. Yet his hand was on the plough, working hard to achieve all he believed God was asking him to do.

QUICK PRAYER:
Give me the courage to dare to
ask and watch Your favor. Amen.

APRIL
30

Facing Stubbornness?

"But Sihon king of Heshbon refused to let us pass through. For the Lord your God had made his spirit stubborn and his heart obstinate in order to give him into your hands, as he has now done." (Deu 2:30)

God has a much better view than we do. Our ways are not His ways. Sometimes He will allow people to go the way they have determined to go. Even this is for a purpose.

All we may see is obstinacy, blindness, and stubbornness, yet God is at work even in the greatest of opposition. How easy would our lives be if we learned just to trust and watch His hand at work?

Resistance is sometimes to be pushed, and other times it is a way to divert us to a higher path. In this case, it was ordained to give victory at a later date. Not all resistance is from the enemy.

QUICK PRAYER:
When I see stubbornness, let me know if it is to overcome or is the work of Your hand. Amen.

MAY
1

Help

"Even if you go and fight courageously in battle, God will overthrow you before the enemy, for God has the power to help or to overthrow." (2 CHR 25:8)

Whose side are you on? What is your motivation? Are you fighting a battle you were never meant to fight? There is a fine line between presumption and faith. Do you want to serve God, or do you want Him to bless your plan? One is true Christianity, the other another form of paganism.

That does sound harsh, but consider it for a moment. Will we do what He wants us to do, or do we serve Him in order to have our agenda met? The Word says to "seek first His kingdom" (Mat 6:33), and then we will get all the other things we need.

He has the power to help or to overthrow; let's not treat our call lightly.

QUICK PRAYER:
Help. Amen.

Stewardship

"For from him and through him and for him are all things. To him be the glory forever! Amen." (ROM 11:36)

Wow, here it is; the core of our reason for being, for serving, for Him, all that we have, all that we are, every blessing, every day. All comes from Him. We barely grasp the true meaning of what it is to be a son or daughter of the King.

All things were created for Him, and by Him, that He will be glorified forever. If all that we have is His, it should all be dedicated to Him, for His use. What do we have in our hand that we would struggle to give away? Where is the waste in resources, in time, in finances?

If only we would view our lives from an eternal perspective, how different would our world be?

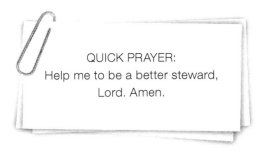

QUICK PRAYER:
Help me to be a better steward,
Lord. Amen.

MAY

3

A Place of Provision

"So Abraham called that place The Lord Will Provide. And to this day it is said, 'On the mountain of the Lord it will be provided.'" (GEN 22:14)

He has the cattle on a thousand hills. Our Father owns all things; there is no shortage in Him, no economic downturn, and no lack. He is the all-sufficient one, the God of more than enough. There is power in that name, the name "The Lord will provide."

He is faithful, and He will meet your need. Our hope is in Him, our trust is in Him, and our provision is in Him. Let's take a moment to be thankful for what we already have, grateful for His past provision, and expectant for our current needs.

We have so many needs in so many areas, yet He is fully aware of all we need and will need in the future, and He has promised to provide.

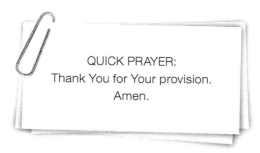

QUICK PRAYER:
Thank You for Your provision.
Amen.

No Lack

"He led you through the vast and dreadful wilderness, that thirsty and waterless land, with its venomous snakes and scorpions. He brought you water out of hard rock." (Deu 8:15)

If we crashed in a desert, how would we survive? It would be hot, arid, and dangerous. Yet God led, fed, and protected a vast army of people for 40 years in the midst of all that danger. They were watered from a rock, fed daily, and protected. Their shoes didn't wear out, and even when they ungratefully demanded meat, it turned up in bountiful abundance.

There is no lack in God. He will provide all our needs according to His riches in glory. I say it again; there is no lack in God—none!

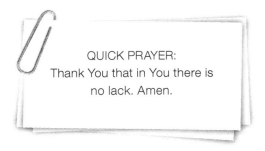

QUICK PRAYER:
Thank You that in You there is no lack. Amen.

MAY
5

Sustenance

"For forty years you sustained them in the wilderness; they lacked nothing, their clothes did not wear out nor did their feet become swollen." (NEH 9:21)

In some seasons, we feel like it will not end. Maybe you have been through a long time of struggling—a long time of waiting for God to answer. Life can be hard sometimes; I am well aware of that. God's answers can seem to be held back for an unreasonable time. But if we have engaged our faith and trusted in His timing, we will see the hand of God move on our behalf.

In the meantime, sometimes we will need to press into Him and ask for Him to sustain us. In Him there is no lack. The Israelites in the desert lacked nothing as He sustained them.

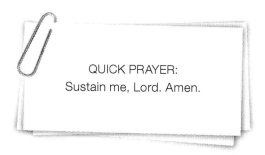

QUICK PRAYER:
Sustain me, Lord. Amen.

Timing

"I will send you such a blessing in the sixth year that the land will yield enough for three years." (Lev 25:21)

God can take what you have and multiply it when it is surrendered to Him. The timing will be according to His agenda, not yours. We live in an instant gratification society, where now is the required timeframe.

Maybe you have been waiting on God and working toward an outcome that seems to be delayed. Do not give up hope, but trust in Him to ensure the right timing. Often it is not you but all the other people and circumstances that need to line up to God's purposes.

But know this: He can vastly multiply what you have to go well beyond natural provision. Take time to hear from Him again, discern His timing, and watch Him multiply what you have surrendered to Him.

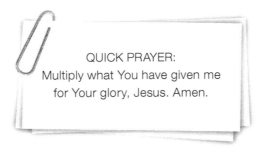

QUICK PRAYER:
Multiply what You have given me
for Your glory, Jesus. Amen.

MAY
7

Over the Top

"So Simon Peter climbed back into the boat and dragged the net ashore. It was full of large fish, 153, but even with so many the net was not torn." (Joh 21:11)

I love this Scripture for two quite distinct reasons. First, it is because God is an abundant provider. The nets weren't full of just enough for the day. They weren't just normal, small fish. They were large—big, fat, juicy, large fish, and in abundance.

Is this what we expect for our workplace? Why not? Are we not in God's service? Are we not appointed and anointed for a purpose? Has not God appointed us to serve where we are? Is He not the same yesterday, today, and forever?

The second aspect is that despite this massive haul of fish, the nets were not damaged. God can enlarge our capacity for a harvest, whether that is financially or as fishers of men. We and our businesses can become the vessels that can contain an abundance of all God has for us.

QUICK PRAYER:
As you bless me, Lord, enlarge
my capacity. Amen.

Faithful in Hard Times

"To deliver them from death and keep them alive in famine."
(Psa 33:19)

He is faithful. He is faithful. He is faithful. I say it again: He is faithful. He will not let you suffer, and He will deliver you from harm. We need to sometimes stand on the promises of God and declare the victory He has already done.

These promises are yes and amen, regardless of the circumstances, the times we live in, the environment, the economy, or the political status. He is our deliverer and our salvation—our ever-present help in a time of need. Speak to those circumstances that seem to overwhelm you, and command them to submit to the Word of God. His strength will sustain you, and His promises are always true.

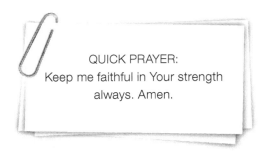

QUICK PRAYER:
Keep me faithful in Your strength
always. Amen.

MAY
9

Good Fear

"Fear the Lord, you his holy people, for those who fear him lack nothing." (Psa 34:9)

Is God some big, overbearing parent Who needs to be appeased? Is He a harsh taskmaster Who demands obedience and waits to punish any error? No, no, and no. We serve a loving heavenly Father Who sent His only Son to die in our place. There is no greater love than His for us.

Yet He remains the Creator of the universe, Whose footstool is the earth. He spoke all that is into being with a word. He has always been, omnipotent and omnipresent. Our small minds cannot begin to imagine His overwhelming size, power, and strength.

Let's not let His love cloud our awe and sense of fear; that holy fear that is based in respect and acknowledgment of who He really is.

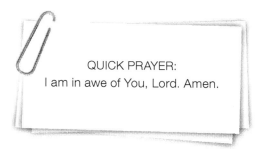

QUICK PRAYER:
I am in awe of You, Lord. Amen.

God's Riches

"Whatever you have learned or received or heard from me, or seen in me—put it into practice. And the God of peace will be with you." (PHI 4:9)

We have learned from God, received from Him, and heard from Him. When we study His Word or hear His still, small voice, we have seen Him. What do we do with these words, impressions, feelings, and instructions? We are exhorted to put them into practice. We need to apply what we have seen of God into our lives so we may be transformed to become more like Him. The more like Him we are, the more effective we will be in the kingdom, the more fruit we will demonstrate, and the closer we will be to being all we can be.

And the outcome according to this Scripture is not the peace of God but something better: the God of peace will be with us.

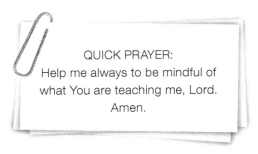

QUICK PRAYER:
Help me always to be mindful of
what You are teaching me, Lord.
Amen.

MAY
11

True Contentment

"I know what it is to be in need, and I know what it is to have plenty. I have learned the secret of being content in any and every situation, whether well fed or hungry, whether living in plenty or in want." (Phi 4:12)

What is true contentment? What would it take for you to feel truly content? We tend to think of that in terms of material possessions, relationships, and circumstances. Paul, who was shipwrecked, beaten, stoned, and jailed, among other great experiences, is talking about something much deeper—a peace that goes beyond all understanding, beyond circumstance and experience. It is a contentment that can only be supernatural in origin.

Imagine being so close to God that all else pales into insignificance. All becomes a shadow, truly in context against the all-powerful light of a totally radiant God. The closer we get to Him, the more content we will be. He is the only certainty, the only constant, and the only place of true contentment.

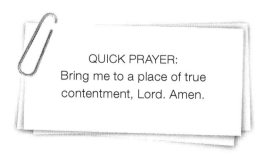

QUICK PRAYER:
Bring me to a place of true
contentment, Lord. Amen.

Why Worry?

"Therefore I tell you, do not worry about your life, what you will eat or drink; or about your body, what you will wear. Is not life more than food, and the body more than clothes?" (MAT 6:25)

We are human, aren't we? We who profess to be spiritually minded actually struggle with all manner of things. The pull of this world and its cares is strong. Jesus said, "Don't worry about it. I've got it covered." The phrase, "Don't worry, be happy" may be flippant, but it has more than a passing dose of truth in it. Do we trust our heavenly Father to provide? By worrying, we are saying that we don't.

We need to discipline our minds and talk to our spirits, reassuring them that God is in control and will provide for our every need. We should focus on what He is concerned with—the advancement of His kingdom.

Seek these things, and let Him worry about what we will wear, what we will eat, and dare I say, what we will drive and where we will live.

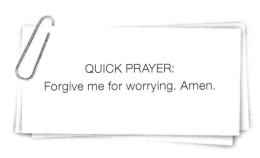

QUICK PRAYER:
Forgive me for worrying. Amen.

MAY

13

God Owns Everything

"To the Lord your God belong the heavens, even the highest heavens, the earth and everything in it." (Deu 10:14)

What do we really own? All we have is God's. We are merely stewards who will, one day, give account for what we have done with that which we were entrusted. Our bank statements will show where our hearts are, but stewardship goes beyond the financial. We all have talents, gifts, and abilities. How are we developing and maximizing the impact of what has been given to us? Do we work with excellence and with a sober realization that God is in all, owns all, and will require a return? Do we allocate time effectively for our entire ministry, at home, work, and church?

These are big questions, but there is only one answer. It is all His, and that perspective changes everything.

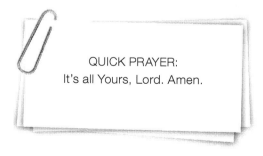

QUICK PRAYER:
It's all Yours, Lord. Amen.

The Origin of Wealth

"Moreover, when God gives someone wealth and possessions, and the ability to enjoy them, to accept their lot and be happy in their toil—this is a gift of God." (Ecc 5:19)

Where do wealth and possessions come from? From our hard work? We would toil in vain without God. It is He who gives us the ability to create wealth and His hand that distributes blessing. Alongside material possessions sometimes come a priceless gift —one that eludes so many who do not know God and many who do.

There is the gift of an ability to enjoy wealth. The wealthiest people are not the happiest. The enjoyment of what we have comes as a gift from God.

The second part of that blessing is a release from striving and looking for the next thing. The trap of materialism is the unending cycle of desire and dissatisfaction. Enjoy, accept, and be happy; it's a great gift.

QUICK PRAYER:
Allow me to enjoy what You have given me, Jesus. Amen.

MAY

15

Wealth Is a Blessing

"The Lord has blessed my master abundantly, and he has become wealthy. He has given him sheep and cattle, silver and gold, male and female servants, and camels and donkeys." (GEN 24:35)

Do not be ashamed of the financial blessings God has bestowed on you. It is He who blesses with wealth in all its forms. If you are struggling, do not be ashamed to ask for His blessing. He is not a stingy God. God is an abundant God—the God of more than enough.

Take a moment to thank Him for all that He has given you. Take a close look around, and you will see all that He has bestowed on you. Use your wealth wisely, submit it to God, and be obedient to His promptings, but enjoy what He has given you to enjoy.

QUICK PRAYER:
Thank You that wealth is a blessing. Please bless me in my finances. Amen.

MAY
16

Success

"In everything he did he had great success, because the Lord was with him." (1 Sam 18:14)

How is your business going? If you are working for another, how is your workplace going? Have you invited God and His blessing into your business? Success comes from Him.

I have seen Him turn around the worst of circumstances. He can move in a commercial environment that is almost beyond redemption and restore profitability, growth, and success.

Each win we have, each sale we get, and every order that comes through the door has contributed to our success, and it has all been ordained by God. If we truly understood that truth, I wonder how thankful and prayerful we would be.

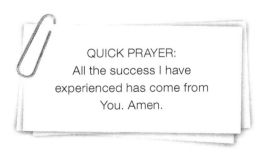

QUICK PRAYER:
All the success I have
experienced has come from
You. Amen.

MAY
17

How Do I Get Exalted?

"Wealth and honor come from you; you are the ruler of all things. In your hands are strength and power to exalt and give strength to all." (1 Chr 29:12)

If there is one truth in business that I have come to understand, it is this: do it God's way, and let Him take care of the consequences. He is in control. Sometimes in the cut and thrust of a brutal commercial world, we forget that truth. But He is and always will be. His ways are not our ways.

Sometimes we all need to stop, pray, and understand His way in a circumstance. Often it is the opposite of how we react. What will people say? Will I miss out on that promotion, deal, or sale? No, God is not only in control; it is also He who exalts, He who promotes, and He who allocates deals. Plus you are given the strength to stand while waiting for the answer from heaven. Now that is a good deal!

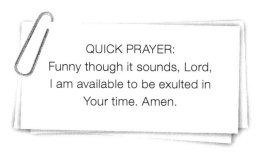

QUICK PRAYER:
Funny though it sounds, Lord,
I am available to be exulted in
Your time. Amen.

A Big Promise

"Therefore wisdom and knowledge will be given you. And I will also give you wealth, possessions and honor, such as no king who was before you ever had and none after you will have." (2 Chr 1:12)

Now that is an impressive list. Is there anyone out there who wouldn't like a piece of that blessing? Solomon asked for wisdom and knowledge and got wealth, possessions, and honor thrown in for free. I don't think they were an addition; I think maybe they were an outcome or a consequence of the first two. The wisdom and knowledge applied led to honor, wealth, and possessions.

Yet the wisdom and knowledge that led to these outcomes was still a gift. Therefore, they need to be spiritually discerned and received. It is our spiritual life that becomes manifest in our physical existence. Our prayer life, insights, and anointing will deliver a physical manifestation of God's blessings and promises. This makes a brief quiet time more appealing, doesn't it?

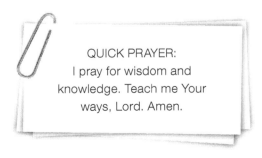

QUICK PRAYER:
I pray for wisdom and knowledge. Teach me Your ways, Lord. Amen.

Your Bit

"Have you not put a hedge around him and his household and everything he has? You have blessed the work of his hands, so that his flocks and herds are spread throughout the land."
(JOB 1:10)

God has placed a hedge of protection around our businesses, if He has been invited to do so. Even when we haven't, there is still grace in His protection. An unfettered attack by our very real enemy would be horrific beyond all imagination. He is a wonderful provider and protector.

But there is a part we need to play. It is one of application, diligence, conscientiousness, and plain old hard work. It is the work of our hands that will be blessed and grow our wealth, revenues, and profit. Two farmers were praying for rain, but one was plowing while he prayed. Guess who got the harvest? Rain fell on both, but one had his hand on the plough and was able to contain God's blessing.

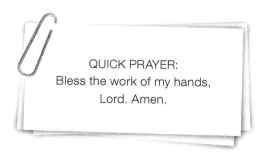

QUICK PRAYER:
Bless the work of my hands,
Lord. Amen.

Restoration

"After Job had prayed for his friends, the Lord restored his fortunes and gave him twice as much as he had before." (Job 42:10)

Have you been through a tough time? Have you had a financial failure, even lost everything? In our populist theology, some will place you in the camp of the apostate. Fortunately, God is not as shallow.

He is the Restorer, the Blesser, and the One who lifts up. There is a new day, a new season, and in God's economy, the surrendered wounds of struggle will be healed and the lessons learned transform into wisdom. The Godliest people I know carry a few scars and have walked a road of ups and downs. They have seen God move in all aspects of life's journey.

We may not have all the answers, but we know Someone Who does. Press into the Restorer of souls and fortunes.

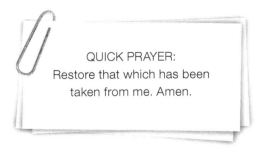

QUICK PRAYER:
Restore that which has been
taken from me. Amen.

MAY
21

A Place of Abundance

"You let people ride over our heads; we went through fire and water, but you brought us to a place of abundance." (Psa 66:12)

It is hard to understand how a loving God would allow things to happen that we wouldn't want to go through. Often He allows circumstances to occur, but always for a reason, always with an outcome, and always to a place of restoration.

Tough places are by definition tough. In this Scripture, they went through the mill, *but...*I love that word. How often do we see His hand in times of struggle and strife? *But* God, *but* He, *but* then. We can experience hope in the midst of turmoil and deliverance to a place of peace, safety, and abundance.

QUICK PRAYER:
Thank You that there is an end
to the tough places and a place
of rest is coming. Amen.

Pray for Success

"Lord, save us! Lord, grant us success!" (Psa 118:25)

Is God interested in our success? Yes He is. I am not sure what it is in us that seems reluctant to ask Him for it. Is it pride that we can do it ourselves? Is it a failure to understand where success ultimately comes from? Perhaps it is a notion that we don't deserve better or that it is presumptuous to ask.

Often I think we are being judged by our own motives, but if we waited for them to be pure, we would never get anything done. Whatever it is, let us lay it down and pick up the biblical understanding that we need to ask for success, for blessing, and for His favor. Let's pray not with human understanding and reticence but in a biblical way—one of total surrender, obedience, and reliance.

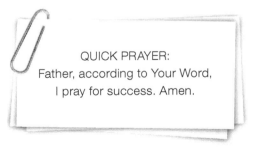

QUICK PRAYER:
Father, according to Your Word,
I pray for success. Amen.

MAY
23

Takeaways

"Naked I came from my mother's womb, and naked I will depart. The Lord gave and the Lord has taken away; may the name of the Lord be praised." (JOB 1:21)

A God that takes away as well as gives? I am not sure that fits with our individualistic, self-centered, post-modern, positive thinking, lifestyle oriented, materialistic, and capitalist view of God. Have we constructed an idol for ourselves? Do we expect Him to do our bidding? How easily can faith become presumption?

We are here a few short years. It is an insignificant speck in time, yet we demand of an eternal God a conformity to our expectations. Sometimes we will not understand from an eternal perspective. Sometimes it will look like God has done us wrong. He gives, and He takes away. Will we still serve Him? Yes, for in Him are the answers to all things and eternal life in Christ.

QUICK PRAYER:
Thank You that You give and that You take away in Your wisdom. Amen.

MAY
24

Bad Times

"When times are good, be happy; but when times are bad, consider this: God has made the one as well as the other. Therefore, no one can discover anything about their future." (Ecc 7:14)

Much though we don't like to admit it, we have good times and bad. Some say it is not acting in faith to admit this. My Bible tells me God is in all things, in all times, both the good and the bad. Here it specifically says God has made both.

Enjoy the good, and work with God in the bad. "Come to Jesus, and everything will go well" is not the gospel. He will walk with us and give us the strength to endure, persevere, fight when required, and overcome when we need to. He is with us always, good and bad, and will always be with us and never forsake us, giving us all we need all the time.

QUICK PRAYER:
Thank You that You are with me in the good and the bad, Holy Spirit. Amen.

MAY

25

Restoration

"'At that time I will gather you; at that time I will bring you home. I will give you honor and praise among all the peoples of the earth when I restore your fortunes before your very eyes,' says the Lord." (Zep 3:20)

God is in the restoration business. He can and does restore hearts, lives, families, and fortunes. He can restore your business when all seems lost. Lives get changed when He is around.

Sometimes He can even restore before your very eyes healings, miracles, radical restoration, Godly reconstruction, and instant reconciliation. Nothing is beyond God's ability to restore—no person, no business, and no situation.

The Bible is full of God "suddenly" doing something. Just when you least suspect it, just when it is at the seemingly lost point, God intervenes. He is never late, but He is, for whatever reason, very rarely early either; and our faith is stretched accordingly.

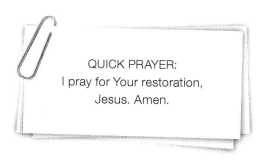

QUICK PRAYER:
I pray for Your restoration,
Jesus. Amen.

MAY
26

Pride and Prejudice

"The Lord tears down the house of the proud, but he sets the widow's boundary stones in place." (PRO 15:25)

We are not proud, are we? Maybe we are just proud of our humility. Pride comes in many forms. Are we self-reliant or too proud to ask? Do we feel a sense of entitlement in our roles at work? Surely it is with the work of our hands that have built this business, family, wealth, or whatever just came into your mind.

When our pride affects our thinking, it will ultimately impact our lives and those in our sphere of influence. He will protect us and the people in our lives by tearing down what is built on pride. Look at your heart, and examine it before God. It is better for us to deal with pride than fall into a sin with consequences.

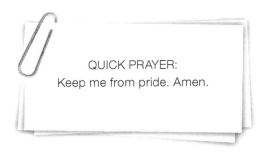

QUICK PRAYER:
Keep me from pride. Amen.

MAY

27

Authority

"The highest heavens belong to the Lord, but the earth he has given to mankind." (Psa 115:16)

I do have a soft spot for environmentalists. They tend to have a different worldview and often a different political agenda than I do, but we have one view in common: we do not own the earth but are just stewards of it. Avoiding damage, correcting wrongs, and increasing awareness of ecological issues all are positive because we have a duty to care for God's creation.

The earth is a gift, and a somewhat fragile one at that. Why not shed our differences and make sure we pass on this incredible gift to our children in better shape than it is right now?

Those who want to protect God's creation, even if they don't call it that, are doing a good thing and should be encouraged. It is the politicization of the agenda and the often radically liberal views that have hijacked a worthy endeavor.

QUICK PRAYER:
Help me to be aware of the
need to steward the planet well.
Amen.

Entrusted

"Again, it will be like a man going on a journey, who called his servants and entrusted his wealth to them." (MAT 25:14)

The resources we have as individuals, and in companies we own or work for, are merely entrusted to us. We don't really own them; they are on loan to us. A return is required both in physical and spiritual terms. Are we good stewards? Do we exercise wisdom and reject the sense of entitlement that so often pervades our thinking? It is an honor to serve the King and to deal well and wisely with all He has entrusted into our care.

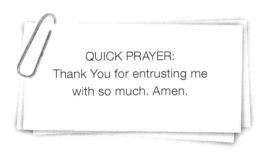

QUICK PRAYER:
Thank You for entrusting me
with so much. Amen.

MAY
29

Trust

"If I preach voluntarily, I have a reward; if not voluntarily, I am simply discharging the trust committed to me." (1 Cor 9:17)

As we go about our daily business, we are often so intent on the task that we don't take the time to consider the circumstances of those around us. We are surrounded by people who may be struggling, and dealing with all sorts of family, health, or financial issues.

Going beyond the physical, what about spiritual wellbeing? There is an eternity to live and only one way in. We literally hold the keys to eternal life. Do we believe that? Then what stops us from sharing the good news with others? Pride? Is it what people will think? Will we really let that stand between someone and eternity?

Ask God to open your eyes to those around you. Somewhere in your world today is someone who needs to hear some truth, and the truth shall set them free.

QUICK PRAYER:
Lead me to someone who
needs to hear about You today.
Amen.

Ownership

"In the same way, those of you who do not give up everything you have cannot be my disciples." (LUK 14:33)

What does it mean to give up everything? To me it is an attitude of the heart—a position of yielding and surrender, of obedience, and of willingness to lay everything down. We are to commit to God all we have, all we do, and all we are.

Commit it all into His hands and it becomes anointed, powerful in His Kingdom, and sanctified for a greater purpose. Moses only had a staff, yet God used it to lead a nation through miracle after miracle. The question He was asked was, "What do you have in your hand?" What do we have in our hands? Let's give it all to God and see what He can do.

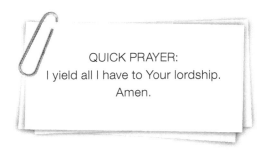

QUICK PRAYER:
I yield all I have to Your lordship.
Amen.

MAY
31

Exchange

"Without delay he called them, and they left their father Zebedee in the boat with the hired men and followed him."
(MAR 1:20)

Will we be ready for a word from God? Do we spend any time with Him to allow us to hear? An instruction from God can come suddenly, swiftly, and without warning. We would do well to spend time with Him and to become familiar with hearing His voice.

Often we will need to act in the confidence that we have heard from Him. Our hearts should be tuned and our lives surrendered so that when we hear, we will be obedient to His Word and act swiftly. What could we accomplish if we were truly surrendered to God?

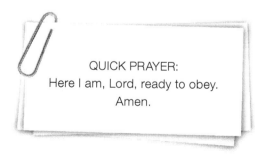

QUICK PRAYER:
Here I am, Lord, ready to obey.
Amen.

Faithfulness

"Now it is required that those who have been given a trust must prove faithful." (1 Cor 4:2)

We have been entrusted with a lot. We have the words of eternal life. An experience of a loving heavenly Father and the Holy Spirit indwells us. We have been given talents, gifts, and abilities to serve, worship, and lead at work.

We have been blessed with resources, wealth, time, family, fellowship, friends, and so much else. What will we do with all we have been entrusted with? Let's be found faithful and proven to be so.

This means an application of purposeful thought and prayer as well as the practical actions that have to be taken to be faithful. It is not an intent but a series of actions that demonstrates an internal condition.

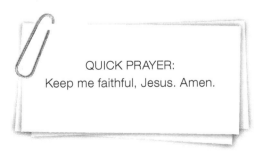

QUICK PRAYER:
Keep me faithful, Jesus. Amen.

JUNE

2

Do

"It will be good for that servant whose master finds him doing so when he returns." (Mat 24:46)

Faith is one thing, but it is actions that really count. Works are evidence of faith. Faith without works is dead (Jam 2:17). Some believers could do well to stop talking about it and get on with doing it. We have so much teaching and input, how about a little output? How about a lot of output? Of those who have been given much, much will be required.

Work is intrinsically good; a business does not need to justify its existence through support of nonbusiness outcomes. However, all we called to be, and to do, needs to be done well and in keeping with God's principles.

Our lives should be evidence of an encounter with the living God—transformed and unrecognizable from what they were.

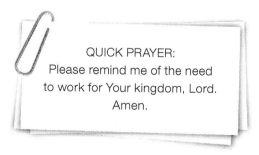

QUICK PRAYER:
Please remind me of the need
to work for Your kingdom, Lord.
Amen.

Intimacy

"His master replied, 'Well done, good and faithful servant! You have been faithful with a few things; I will put you in charge of many things. Come and share your master's happiness!'" (MAT 25:21)

Would you like to share in the happiness of God? He is the Creator of all happiness, pleasure, and joy. Shared happiness is sign of intimacy and of a close relationship. What a beautiful picture of our Father's love for us.

It is out of an understanding of that love and the overwhelming gift of His sacrifice that our faith and works are grounded. It is not out of appeasing an angry, capricious being but in faithfully serving a loving and giving God.

Plus, when we have been proven faithful with a little, we will be given much more. It is spiritual principle that is outworked so clearly in our work in the marketplace.

QUICK PRAYER:
I want to share in Your
happiness, Holy Spirit. Amen.

JUNE
4

Multiplied

"For whoever has will be given more, and they will have abundance. Whoever does not have, even what they have will be taken from them." (MAT 25:29)

Ouch, this is quite a warning. We all have been given a set of gifts, talents, and personality and an allocation of time and resources. The question is, how have we taken what we have been given and applied it to being effective in the kingdom of God? Have we reaped a return from what we have been given?

These are big questions. Do we have adequate answers? It is worth taking some time to take what we have been given before God and ask Him for His wisdom in applying what we have to seeing His kingdom established.

QUICK PRAYER:
Help me to be faithful with what
You have entrusted to me, Lord.
Amen.

Wise

"The Lord answered, 'Who then is the faithful and wise manager, whom the master puts in charge of his servants to give them their food allowance at the proper time?'" (Luk 12:42)

Wisdom is not some high ideal that is gained by sitting in a cave in a desolate place. It is not a state that only a few who study forever will ultimately gain. Wisdom is a practical application of knowledge, understanding, and revelation to enable God's kingdom to be advanced.

The Word says if you lack wisdom, ask and you will receive all you need. That is not a bad promise. There is no problem that God does not have an answer for. Seek Him and you will know what to do.

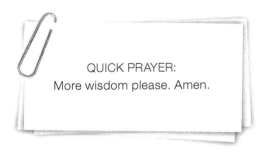

QUICK PRAYER:
More wisdom please. Amen.

JUNE

6

Paying a Price

"When her owners realized that their hope of making money was gone, they seized Paul and Silas and dragged them into the marketplace to face the authorities." (ACT 16:19)

Whether we like to admit it or not, we often find ourselves serving God for what we can get rather than who He is. This is reflected in our prayers that are often, "Help me, I want something."

There are consequences for following Jesus that none of us would choose. We will get ridiculed and sometimes persecuted. We can take some comfort in the fact that Jesus was continually being taken to task and ultimately killed.

When you receive opposition, you should take it as a compliment. Our enemy only has limited resources, and when he allocates some to your life, you must be having an impact.

QUICK PRAYER:
I know I will pay a price for standing with You. Help me be strong and protect my heart at that time. Amen.

JUNE
7

Obedience

"However, there need be no poor people among you, for in the land the Lord your God is giving you to possess as your inheritance, he will richly bless you." (Deu 15:4)

Hang on, that surely can't be right. If we have God's blessing, there will be no poverty. He will richly provide for all our needs and for those around us. It is God's heart that there be no poverty. Let's bear in mind the heart of God.

Here is an unpopular question for you: how much of what God has given us have we set aside to meet the needs of the poor? We are rich beyond all measure if we take a global view. Are we eating the bread He destined to provide for others?

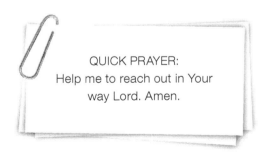

QUICK PRAYER:
Help me to reach out in Your
way Lord. Amen.

JUNE

8

Pay Attention Now

"The Lord will make you the head, not the tail. If you pay attention to the commands of the Lord your God that I give you this day and carefully follow them, you will always be at the top, never at the bottom." (Deu 28:13)

Wow! What a promise. We will always be at the top, never at the bottom. We will be at the head, not the tail. That means we are the initiators. We are the ones who will dictate terms. We are the ones in control. We are leaders, not followers. Is that our experience? It is not mine—not all the time. So what is the condition of the promise? We will be the head if we pay attention to the commands of the Lord and carefully follow them. If we do this and stand in faith, we will receive all that God has for us. We will no longer be pushed around by circumstances but living in victory.

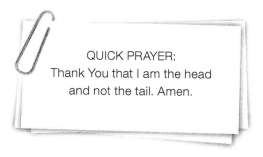

QUICK PRAYER:
Thank You that I am the head
and not the tail. Amen.

Seeker

"He sought God during the days of Zechariah, who instructed him in the fear of God. As long as he sought the Lord, God gave him success." (2 Chr 26:5)

Sometimes we expect all things good to fall into our laps. We get lazy in our quiet times. We get slack in our reading of God's Word. Then things start going wrong in our world, and we wonder why. There are times when we need to up our game, press in, and really seek God.

If this is you right now, why not make a commitment to seek Him this week? Maybe a fast is in order. Set aside time to really seek Him. You will be glad you did. God will ultimately give you success.

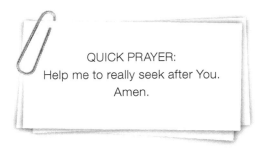

QUICK PRAYER:
Help me to really seek after You.
Amen.

JUNE

10

Be Wholehearted

"In everything that he undertook in the service of God's temple and in obedience to the law and the commands, he sought his God and worked wholeheartedly. And so he prospered." (2 Chr 31:21)

How committed is committed? If you are anything like me, you will have times when you are just going through the motions. Oh, it is just me, is it? Here is a challenge to be wholehearted. Let's stir up our spirits and pledge once again to make a full commitment to God's will in our lives. His promise if we do according to His Word is that we will prosper, and we can all do with greater measure of God's blessing.

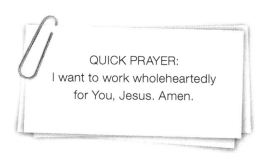

QUICK PRAYER:
I want to work wholeheartedly
for You, Jesus. Amen.

Tough Choice

"This day I call the heavens and the earth as witnesses against you that I have set before you life and death, blessings and curses. Now choose life, so that you and your children may live." (Deu 30:19)

Every day we face choices. They may be small, seemingly insignificant, tiny choices. Do we do the right thing or the wrong thing? No one will notice, we tell ourselves. No one will ever know. It seems like such a small thing. Everyone else is doing it. How wrong can it really be? Is it really that important to make a stand? What will people think?

Small choices lead to big choices. Small variations end up being big deviations, and the whole world will witness our choices. Our lives are just a sum of the choices we make. What will you choose?

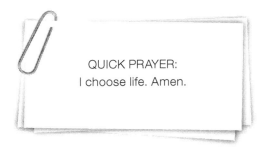

QUICK PRAYER:
I choose life. Amen.

JUNE
12

Priorities

"'You expected much, but see, it turned out to be little. What you brought home, I blew away. Why?' declares the Lord Almighty. 'Because of my house, which remains a ruin, while each of you is busy with your own house.'" (HAG 1:9)

We do not expect God to oppose us. He is for us and not against us. However, what the Scripture demonstrates is a priority. How engaged are we in our local church? The reality that is funding from God's generous provision to us should also help build His house.

The discipline of putting aside a fixed sum and using that to meet the needs of God's kingdom, whether that be in his house or not, is one well worth having.

We are called to serve not only in the marketplace but also the local community. While sharing the financial burden, using our prosperity to meet the needs of others, and financing the kingdom of God, we also need to be generous with our time and build the local house of God. Then we can rest assured that He will provide for our house.

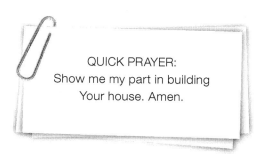

QUICK PRAYER:
Show me my part in building
Your house. Amen.

JUNE
13

Big Price to Pay

"The shepherds are senseless and do not inquire of the Lord; so they do not prosper and all their flock is scattered." (Jer 10:21)

There are two ways we can lead our lives: we can rely on our own understanding and wisdom, or we can inquire of God. When we lean on our own understanding, we are trusting in our own resources and wisdom.

While we are given a brain and have a duty to apply it to situations, the foundation of our reasoning should be the Word of God. If we are immersed in His Word and walk with Him intimately, we will have the mind of Christ.

The shepherds were senseless because they did not inquire of the Lord. The result was a lack of prosperity, and what they had was scattered.

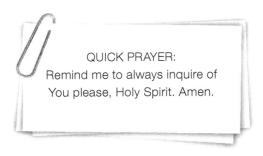

QUICK PRAYER:
Remind me to always inquire of
You please, Holy Spirit. Amen.

JUNE

14

Perspective

"Humility is the fear of the Lord; its wages are riches and honor and life." (PRO 22:4)

If people are described as humble, how would you perceive them? Would you see them as strong? Would you see them as powerful? Perhaps because of the denigration of what it is to be humble, we have a perception that humility equals weakness.

True humility is the fear of the Lord. It is not only an intellectual assent to the salvation of Christ but a submission to His lordship. When we align ourselves with God's Word and with the King of Kings, we are humble. When we agree with what He says about us, we are humble. When we trust in what He says rather than the circumstances we see, we are humble.

And the wages of humility? They are riches and life. Not a bad outcome.

QUICK PRAYER:
Keep me humble. Amen.

JUNE
15

Accountability

"So he called him in and asked him, 'What is this I hear about you? Give an account of your management, because you cannot be manager any longer." (Luk 16:2)

We are all accountable to someone. We all have a boss, a board, a manager, or someone who has authority over us. There are no lone rangers in the kingdom of God. There is wisdom in community and in the application of accountability.

Spiritual accountability for practical reality makes a lot of common sense. Very few of us want to have accountability, and yet part of the wisdom in walking with God is surrounding ourselves with people who will hold us accountable.

God is into accountability. One day we will all stand before Him and give an account. Yes, if we are born-again, we will not be held responsible for our sin, yet we will be held accountable for what we have done with what we were given.

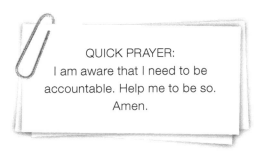

QUICK PRAYER:
I am aware that I need to be accountable. Help me to be so.
Amen.

JUNE

16

Bills

"Let no debt remain outstanding, except the continuing debt to love one another, for whoever loves others has fulfilled the law." (Rom 13:8)

Sometimes the Scriptures are deliberately vague. We have to dig deep for the truth, and there are layers of understanding. Other times things are so obvious in black-and-white that we almost miss them.

Let no debts remain outstanding. If we look into the ancient text, reference the commentators of the time, seek out all the different interpretations of the Scripture, and assemble it all together, it makes no difference. The Word still says to let no debt remain outstanding.

If you have debts remaining, let them not remain outstanding.

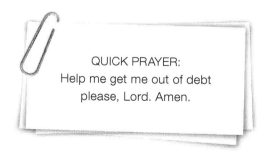

QUICK PRAYER:
Help me get me out of debt
please, Lord. Amen.

Slavery

"The rich rule over the poor, and the borrower is slave to the lender." (PRO 22:7)

I don't think I would like to be a slave. Despite us thinking that it is an ancient trade, there are more slaves on the planet today than there have ever been. It is a tragic industry trading in human misery.

Yet here in Proverbs, a borrower is described as a slave to the lender. The power a master has over a slave has no end. It is a good reminder about God's attitude toward debt. When we are in debt, we are literally owned by the person we are in debt to. Think twice and think again before entering into debt.

Give due heed to this Scripture when you look to enter into any debt contract. When we are in debt, we lose a piece of our freedom.

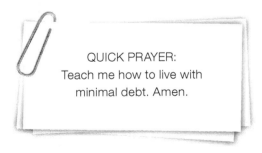

QUICK PRAYER:
Teach me how to live with
minimal debt. Amen.

JUNE
18

The Price of Debt

"The wife of a man from the company of the prophets cried out to Elisha, 'Your servant my husband is dead, and you know that he revered the Lord. But now his creditor is coming to take my two boys as his slaves.'" (2 Kin 4:1)

My God is a generous God. He does supply all my needs. But if I squander his provision, if I am flippant with His generosity, or if I do not have an attitude of stewardship, I will quickly live beyond my means.

The temptation to keep up with the Joneses is a strong one. We live in a material world where we are continually bombarded with messages of the new and the greatest.

While God is fully aware of the society in which we live and what we need to partake in society and be effective, must be careful to be wise with what He has given us. The price we can pay for being out of control and falling into the hands of creditors is too high.

QUICK PRAYER:
I know there is a price to pay for living outside my means. Give me wisdom. Amen.

Prompt Payment

"Do not say to your neighbor, 'Come back tomorrow and I'll give it to you'—when you already have it with you." (Pro 3:28)

I like this description because it demonstrates the heart of God. There is something very right and proper about spontaneously meeting a need. If we have something in hand that can meet a need of others, we shouldn't even hesitate to give.

There is something inherently wrong with having resources and not meeting the need. Even in business, in the brutal cut and thrust of the commercial world, the principles of generosity apply.

If we can pay bills now, why not pay them now? This could cut across the prevailing culture and demonstrate a transformed life. Isn't that what we are supposed to be doing?

QUICK PRAYER:
Help me to be prompt in my
payments. Amen.

JUNE
20

Pay Back

"The wicked borrow and do not repay, but the righteous give generously." (Psa 37:21)

We are called to be in contrast to those around us. If it is considered good practice to borrow and not to repay, then we should give generously. Just because everyone is doing it doesn't mean it is okay to do.

We serve a generous God—One Who gave everything to save us. The material things we have are all His. Everything we have, and everything we are, has come from the hand of a generous God. We are merely stewards of what has been entrusted to us. It is all God's.

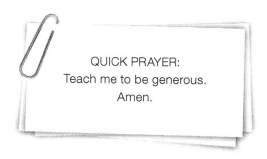

QUICK PRAYER:
Teach me to be generous.
Amen.

Supernatural Provision

"She went and told the man of God, and he said, 'Go, sell the oil and pay your debts. You and your sons can live on what is left.'" (2 Kin 4:7)

There is a spiritual principle that affects our physical existence; we reap what we sow. What we put in, we get out. Often the type of seed we sow is the fruit we reap. These things are the provision of God. Sometimes He goes abundantly beyond all we can think.

When it has all gone horribly wrong and what we have feared has come to pass, God is still able to provide. He may well provide in a truly supernatural fashion. He can open doors no man can shut. He can provide in ways we cannot even imagine. He can provide a way when there is no way.

Let's not forget that He is an omnipotent God. He is the Creator of all things, and He is without limit. He is bigger than our need, and He can and will provide.

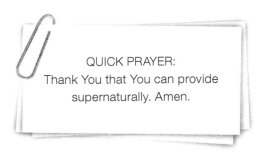

QUICK PRAYER:
Thank You that You can provide
supernaturally. Amen.

JUNE

22

Forgiveness of Debts

"When the neighboring peoples bring merchandise or grain to sell on the Sabbath, we will not buy from them on the Sabbath or on any holy day. Every seventh year we will forgo working the land and will cancel all debts." (Neh 10:31)

We sometimes forget that our economy is not necessarily built on godly principles. While I truly believe that the democratic free-market capitalist system is as good as it gets, there are certain godly principles that are not inherent in the way we do commerce.

In the ancient world, there was a seven-year cycle of forgiving debts. What a wonderful demonstration of forgiveness and grace and mercy. What an acknowledgment that all belongs to God.

We have been forgiven much. Let's not forget where we were when God found us. We who have received mercy should be merciful.

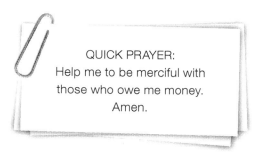

QUICK PRAYER:
Help me to be merciful with
those who owe me money.
Amen.

JUNE
23

Mercy

"Neither of them had the money to pay him back, so he forgave the debts of both. Now which of them will love him more?"
(Luk 7:42)

Those of us who know God are a privileged few. We are sinners saved by grace. Our sin has been washed away. We are clean, redeemed, and sanctified. We have the righteousness of Jesus Christ.

Those who have been forgiven much will love much. We have been forgiven so much. How can we even begin to understand the depth of forgiveness that has been given to us who deserve no forgiveness? How much more should we forgive those around us who sin against us?

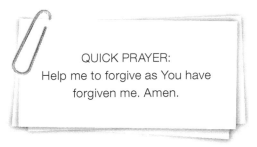

QUICK PRAYER:
Help me to forgive as You have
forgiven me. Amen.

JUNE

24

Schmuck

"One who has no sense shakes hands in pledge and puts up security for a neighbor." (Pro 17:18)

Someone, obviously of Jewish heritage, once said that a guarantor is just a schmuck with a pen. Perhaps this is a somewhat unkind designation, yet quite possibly the sentiment of this Jewish gentleman agrees with the Word of God.

Don't put up security for a neighbor. If you have pledged for another, go now and unshackle yourself from potential disaster. Only you can meet the obligations you promise to another. You cannot guarantee the debts or behaviors of others.

God is quite clear; don't be a schmuck.

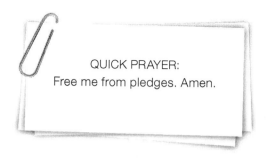

QUICK PRAYER:
Free me from pledges. Amen.

Renegotiate

"My son, if you have put up security for your neighbor, if you have shaken hands in pledge for a stranger, you have been trapped by what you said, ensnared by the words of your mouth." (PRO 6:1–2)

The essence of this proverb occurs a number of times in Scripture. It's obviously an important financial principle, particularly for those of us who are in business.

If we are in onerous contracts or agreements or have guaranteed another entity or person, we need to renegotiate. Don't put off, don't delay, and don't get distracted or be put off by the inconvenience or how it may be perceived; go and get it changed.

The Bible describes it as a trap, that we have been ensnared by the words of our mouth. If it is God's will that we not enter into such an agreement, He will give us a way of escape.

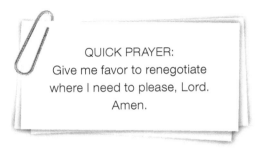

QUICK PRAYER:
Give me favor to renegotiate
where I need to please, Lord.
Amen.

JUNE

26

Advisors

"Plans are established by seeking advice; so if you wage war, obtain guidance." (PRO 20:18)

How often do you think you know best? Often we only think we are right because we haven't heard anything better. Perhaps there is a better way.

When we are embarking on a new venture, making a new plan, or moving in a new direction, there is wisdom in seeking the advice of others. It is pride or haste that stops us from seeking the wisdom of others. When we are reliant on ourselves, we are guaranteed to make the mistakes that others have already made.

There is often wisdom in the collective reasoning of a team of close advisers. Many brains are better than one. When we look at a problem or opportunity from a number of different perspectives, the conclusions we draw are more complete.

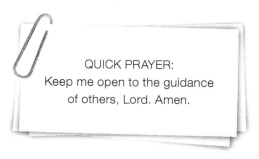

QUICK PRAYER:
Keep me open to the guidance
of others, Lord. Amen.

Take Advice

"Moses listened to his father-in-law and did everything he said." (Exo 18:24)

Don't try to do it all yourself. Do you really think you know it all? God has placed around us people with wisdom, experience, understanding, and insight. Why not take the time to seek some advice?

Take the time to seek godly counsel. You will be glad you did.

If you don't have these kinds of people around you, seek them out. Ask God to provide you with people who will help you in your walk with Him.

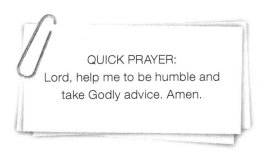

QUICK PRAYER:
Lord, help me to be humble and
take Godly advice. Amen.

JUNE

28

Godly Counsel

"To God belong wisdom and power; counsel and understanding are his." (Job 12:13)

We are plugged into the one Who knows everything. There is nothing He doesn't know. He's never surprised by anything that happens. In Him is all power. All counsel and all understanding are his.

Why, oh why, do we not call on the resources available to us more often? He is Almighty God. He is for us and not against us. He's vitally and intimately interested in all you do at work.

Call on Him today, and see His wisdom, power, counsel, and understanding impact you and your workplace.

QUICK PRAYER:
You are the fount of all wisdom and counsel. Lord, help me in my hour of need. Amen.

JUNE
29

Dreams

"I will praise the Lord, who counsels me; even at night my heart instructs me." (Psa 16:7)

If you are an entrepreneur or an idea person, you may sometimes be called a dreamer. Perhaps you are a contemplative person and maybe this label applies to you also. Take it as a compliment.

God can talk to us through our dreams. Even at night He can impact our lives. If you have a dream, take it to Him, and ask Him what it means. God can guide us during the day and talk to us during the night. The Bible is full of people who heard God in dreams. Don't limit the way that He will talk to you.

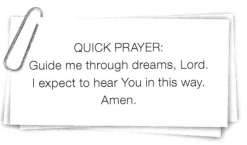

QUICK PRAYER:
Guide me through dreams, Lord.
I expect to hear You in this way.
Amen.

JUNE

30

Wonderful Ideas

"For to us a child is born, to us a son is given, and the government will be on his shoulders. And he will be called Wonderful Counselor, Mighty God, Everlasting Father, Prince of Peace." (Isa 9:6)

There is so much in this one small Scripture. A child is born, a Son is given, the great gift of God. He has authority and rule, and we are called to be subject to Him.

He is described by the Holy Spirit as being a Wonderful Counselor. He is described as the mighty God Creator. He is described as the everlasting Father and the true Son of the Prince of Peace—a wonderful and complete explanation of the Trinity and the aspects of God.

The added bonus is that the Holy Spirit is our counselor, and we walk with Him every day. Here's something truly wonderful—that creativity can flow through us.

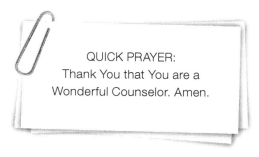

QUICK PRAYER:
Thank You that You are a
Wonderful Counselor. Amen.

Wise Words

"Your statutes are my delight; they are my counselors."
(Psa 119:24)

When we are in the workplace, we'll sometimes be tempted to believe that God is not interested in our workplace. This is just not the case. The words God has written down in the Bible when read by us and imparted to us by the Holy Spirit are life giving.

The scriptural principles laid out by God in the Bible should be our delight. They bring wisdom and understanding and are very much our counselor. When we receive this wisdom, it has no effect if we just understand and acknowledge it. It only has an effect when we act on it and make it a demonstrable part of our lives.

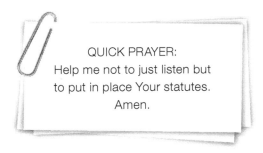

QUICK PRAYER:
Help me not to just listen but
to put in place Your statutes.
Amen.

JULY
2

Parents

"Listen to your father, who gave you life, and do not despise your mother when she is old." (Pro 23:22)

Sometimes we assume that the parents' role is over when the child leaves home. Perhaps we would do well to heed the advice of the Bible that seems to honor a parent's advice for a lot longer time.

While we may not understand this principle, depending on our skill base and the relationship we have with our parents, it is nonetheless a God-ordained decree. They have a lot more life under their belts than we do, and while we may or may not respect their opinions, we would do well to open our ears to their advice based on this principle in God's Word.

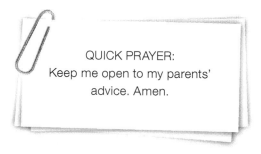

QUICK PRAYER:
Keep me open to my parents'
advice. Amen.

The Gift of Wisdom

"All the kings of the earth sought audience with Solomon to hear the wisdom God had put in his heart." (2 Chr 9:23)

We sometimes see wisdom as an elusive trait. It is merely the practical application of godly insight. The origin of true wisdom is in God. He's the Author and Finisher of our faith. In Him is all wisdom and all insight.

God can grant us wisdom for a particular situation. He can grow wisdom in us through experience, and by learning from Him, we can impart wisdom. Wisdom is a gifting where we intuitively see the practical solutions in the situations that confront us. Whatever way you look at wisdom, it is a good thing, so why not ask God for some today?

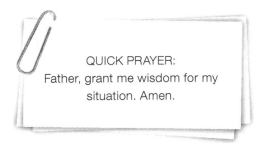

QUICK PRAYER:
Father, grant me wisdom for my situation. Amen.

JULY

4

Wise Company

"Walk with the wise and become wise, for a companion of fools suffers harm." (PRO 13:20)

The people we spend time with will impact our lives. They will either be impacted for good, or they'll be impacted for bad. How would you rate the people you mix with? That sounds like a very harsh judgment or question. And yes, we are called to mix with those who need to know Jesus. There is nothing wrong with this; in fact, there is a lot of good in mixing with those who have yet to come to know Him.

Yet those who are close to us and those we choose to seek advice from will impact our lives. If we want to be wise, it would be prudent to walk with the wise. Be careful to choose the company you keep wisely. This principle is true in our work life as well as our social life.

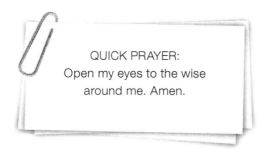

QUICK PRAYER:
Open my eyes to the wise
around me. Amen.

The Wisdom of Age

"But Rehoboam rejected the advice the elders gave him and consulted the young men who had grown up with him and were serving him." (1 Kin 12:8)

Grey hair is a sign of wisdom, or so the Scriptures tell us. I am all in agreement with this the greyer I become myself. More often than not we take it as a sign of irrelevance or not being in touch.

That aside, there is wisdom that comes with age. It is experience that cannot be taught. Youth and enthusiasm are great things. I love the energy around people who are fully engaged, passionate, and youthful. But I have learned over the years that there is a need to balance youthful enthusiasm with the measured contemplation that comes with those who have some years of experience. We should honor the elders in our midst, even if society and in particular commerce does not.

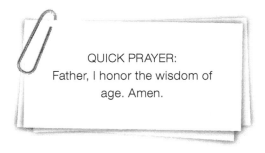

QUICK PRAYER:
Father, I honor the wisdom of age. Amen.

JULY

6

Bad Advice

"The plans of the righteous are just, but the advice of the wicked is deceitful." (Pro 12:5)

Everyone will give you advice if you ask for it. Many will give you advice even if you don't. It is important to look beyond the advice to the one who is giving it. It is by your fruit that you will be known. Look for the fruit of the advisers around you.

There is a need to discern advice in all aspects of your work or business life. It's as much about looking at the source as it is about deciding whether the advice is good or not in its own right. The advice of the wicked will be deceitful even if it looks on the surface like good advice.

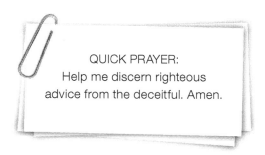

QUICK PRAYER:
Help me discern righteous
advice from the deceitful. Amen.

JULY
7

Deceit

"The heart is deceitful above all things and beyond cure. Who can understand it?" (Jer 17:9)

We are very complex beings. Ask anyone who is married. Often we can't understand even the one we live with and have lived with for many years. It's true that often we don't even understand ourselves.

The complexity of experience, upbringing, motivators, pressures, and stress—even what we eat or how we sleep—creates a volatile and somewhat unpredictable cocktail. Our very hearts can be deceitful and fool even ourselves.

So what can we do? We can trust the God who created us, who understands us completely, who sees us completely, and who loves us completely.

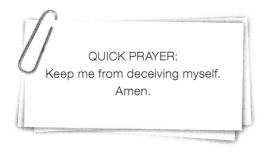

QUICK PRAYER:
Keep me from deceiving myself.
Amen.

JULY

8

Own Up

"Achan replied, 'It is true! I have sinned against the Lord, the God of Israel. This is what I have done.'" (Jos 7:20)

Guilt is a terrible burden. Fear of consequences can be all consuming. There is something cleansing, right, and proper about owning up and facing the consequences of receiving forgiveness.

God will always forgive even when we can't forgive ourselves. His forgiveness knows no bounds. There is nothing you have done, are doing, or will do that is beyond the forgiveness of God. He has already provided for all the forgiveness you will need.

While men may not forgive, God will always, always forgive. Put your confidence in Him, and let Him deal with the consequences. Your conscience will be clean, and God will deal with what happens. You may well pay a human price, but your heart will be free.

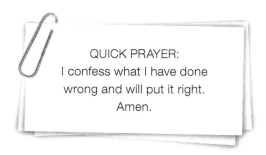

QUICK PRAYER:
I confess what I have done
wrong and will put it right.
Amen.

Be on Your Guard

"The merchant uses dishonest scales and loves to defraud."
(Hos 12:7)

We are all tempted to cut corners at work from time to time. The easy way is often the wrong way. Just because everyone else doing it doesn't make it right. We are called to pay our taxes and be compliant with all legislation, regardless of our views on its validity.

When it comes to our customers, are we providing true value? Do we do what we say, work how we commit to, meet our deadlines, and complete all our work? How can we go even further and walk the extra mile?

God's way should compel us to a higher standard, to the highest standard, as serving Him. Let our reputations as Christians in the marketplace be a demonstration of the transformed life we claim to have received.

QUICK PRAYER:
Keep me on the narrow, true
path, Lord. Forgive me for where
I have cut corners. Amen.

JULY

10

Truth Is a Person

"Jesus answered, "I am the way and the truth and the life. No one comes to the Father except through me." (JOH 14:6)

How important is the truth? In the pressure cooker business lives we lead, shortcuts and 'white lies' are often deemed expedient, or at least understandable.

So how important is the truth really? Jesus described Himself as the truth—the physical manifestation of truth, the ultimate in all truth. That is how we should value the truth. We are called to a different standard where we will honor the truth in deed and in the person of Jesus.

When we speak the truth, we honor God. He is the personification of all truth.

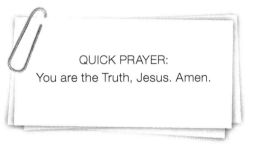

QUICK PRAYER:
You are the Truth, Jesus. Amen.

The Guide

* * *

"But when he, the Spirit of truth, comes, he will guide you into all the truth. He will not speak on his own; he will speak only what he hears, and he will tell you what is yet to come." (Joh 16:13)

Here the Holy Spirit is described as the Spirit of truth. That is yet another pointer to the calling to integrity. So what will He do? He will guide you into all truth. That's right—God will guide you into truth. What sort of truth are we talking about?

The truth that comes from the Father is the ultimate truth. The Spirit will also tell us what is yet to come. Wow, the one who loves and guides us will talk to us about the future. That is His promise.

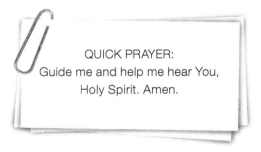

QUICK PRAYER:
Guide me and help me hear You,
Holy Spirit. Amen.

JULY

12

Do Not Lie

"Do not steal. Do not lie. Do not deceive one another." (LEV 19:11)

Here is one of those Scripture that cuts to the chase. It goes beyond any manipulation and tells it like it is. Does it leave any room for doubt? No. Does it leave any room for a minimal offense? No.

It is black and white, clear and simple—don't lie, don't steal, and don't deceive.

That one simple short line convicts us all of sin. If you don't think it applies to you, take a moment and have a reality check. We all fall short of the glory of God, and a man who says he is without sin is a liar.

This applies to our work lives and businesses, just as it does to all other aspects of life. Just because it is a common practice doesn't make it right.

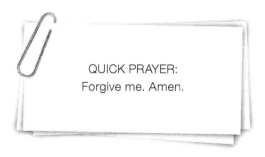

QUICK PRAYER:
Forgive me. Amen.

Take Advantage?

"If you sell land to any of your own people or buy land from them, do not take advantage of each other." (Lev 25:14)

Usually in a deal, one side has an advantage—not always but quite often. The willing buyer and willing seller always have hidden agendas and motivations. While these are usually hidden, sometimes they are not. There may be financial or situational stress causing one party to be vulnerable. It may be a transaction between parties that have a hierarchical relationship or other emotional leverage.

What are we to do in such circumstances? Are we to take the purely commercial view? It is after all a dog-eat-dog world, right? Yes, that is right, but we who have been lifted out of a hopeless situation when we had no leverage should show the mercy we have been shown. Don't take advantage, and let God bless the outcome.

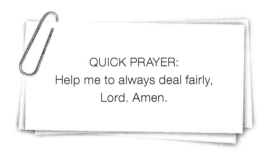

QUICK PRAYER:
Help me to always deal fairly,
Lord. Amen.

JULY
14

The Weight of Truth

"Do not have two differing weights in your bag—one heavy, one light." (DEU 25:13)

This Scripture deals with honesty and integrity—two standards we all know are important to uphold. God is, as usual, black and white regarding the standard required, but here I think we have a scenario where we can take a second look.

The weights referred to were to deceive—one for when selling and one for when buying. But I am sure they were not used in all circumstances. They would be deployed only when the merchant thought he could deceive. It was a way to prey on the weak, the vulnerable, and the inexperienced.

Our challenge is simple. Do we treat all alike, with respect, dignity, and honor? Or do we take advantage of those who are less experienced?

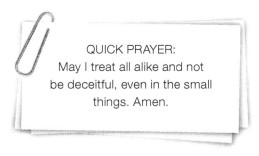

QUICK PRAYER:
May I treat all alike and not
be deceitful, even in the small
things. Amen.

JULY

15

Contentment

"Then some soldiers asked him, 'And what should we do?' He replied, 'Don't extort money and don't accuse people falsely— be content with your pay.'" (LUK 3:14)

We live in a world that constantly demands more. Why have one car when you can have two? Why have the old model when you can have the latest? Upgrade, up-spec, trade up, get the latest, don't miss out, etc. With all these demands on our income, we always want more.

When we have a want for more, our motivations become financial. This can lead to shortcuts and a focus on making more regardless of consequences. Very few people set out to steal, cheat, or damage their families. It is a slow, insidious process.

There is nothing wrong with a profit motive or monetary blessing, but it must be constrained. It is balanced by a generous heart and contentment.

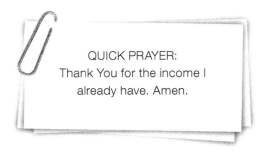

QUICK PRAYER:
Thank You for the income I
already have. Amen.

JULY

16

Judge Yourself

"You, then, who teach others, do you not teach yourself? You who preach against stealing, do you steal?" (ROM 2:21)

It is always easier to preach than practice. At work, do we walk the talk, or do we just expect others to live up to our standards? While we are all given some level of influence in our workplace, we do have a responsibility to apply our message first to ourselves.

It is very, very easy to judge others and very hard to judge ourselves. We already know our excuses. They are, of course, most reasonable and understandable under the circumstances.

The first person who should measure up to what we teach, preach, or proclaim is ourselves. People are also all very well aware of their own shortcomings and may not necessarily benefit from us highlighting them, especially if we are demonstrating the same failing.

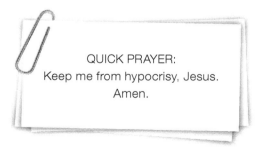

QUICK PRAYER:
Keep me from hypocrisy, Jesus.
Amen.

JULY
17

A High Ideal.

"For it is written: 'Be holy, because I am holy.'" (1 PET 1:16)

To what standard are we called? To what level of purity are we to strive? How good is good enough? There is no judgment because we are declared holy by the one who will judge the world. It is not because we are righteous but because we received the righteousness of Christ—a free gift for any sinner.

The outworking of that is another matter. The impossible is only made possible when we know it is impossible in our hands, but we can do all things through Crist. We will not attain this holiness, but it is the required measure. We can only trust God and let Him work in us to work out His holiness.

Is it a paradox? Yes it is, but a strangely beautiful one.

QUICK PRAYER:
Help me be holy as You are holy.
Only You can truly transform me.
Amen.

JULY
18

Do What Is Right

"This is what the Sovereign Lord says: You have gone far enough, princes of Israel! Give up your violence and oppression and do what is just and right. Stop dispossessing my people, declares the Sovereign Lord." (Eze 45:9)

Justice and righteousness? Are these words we would use regularly in the workplace? I don't think I have heard them uttered recently in any meetings I have been in, yet they are high on God's agenda. He wants to see us walk in them at work.

We are called to do what is just and right. He wants leaders to do the right thing and managers to do the correct thing. They are not necessarily the same thing. Sometimes they are, but it is the way in which they are executed that makes them just and right.

We can bring correction or an alternative view while honoring others, or we can be dogmatic and judgmental. Are you walking in justice and righteousness? It may only be in manner, but God sees the attitudes of the heart.

QUICK PRAYER:
Show me where I am oppressing anyone, and forgive all my shortcomings. Amen.

The Price of Honesty

"What a person desires is unfailing love; better to be poor than a liar." (Pro 19:22)

We all have an innate reaction that will cause us to protect ourselves when under threat. Our first response when we are accused is to deny. We learn to overcome this protective response though the conscious choice to operate in honesty and integrity.

At what point would we lie to save ourselves or our finances? This is a tough question and one hopefully we won't need to know the answer to, but I would doubt many of us would refuse to say a little, tiny, insignificant white lie that wouldn't hurt a fly rather than lose all our finances, our house, car, job, and possessions.

God's view? It is better to be poor than a liar, and honesty is a mark of unfailing love.

QUICK PRAYER:
Keep me honest above all things. Amen.

JULY

20

A Curse

"'Cursed is the cheat who has an acceptable male in his flock and vows to give it, but then sacrifices a blemished animal to the Lord. For I am a great king,' says the Lord Almighty, 'and my name is to be feared among the nations.'" (Mal 1:14)

Through the sacrifice of Jesus, we are freed from the curse of the breach of the Law. We are now subject to grace and the blessing of Abraham because we live by faith.

The essence of this passage is when we promise to give of our best, we should keep our word. In those moments where we feel full of the power of God and sense His presence, we are quick to say we will do this and that and promise to give and achieve or follow a set of standards. We would do well to keep our word or promise what we intend to fulfill. He is Almighty God. If we have that relationship right, we are more likely to keep our word with those around us at work.

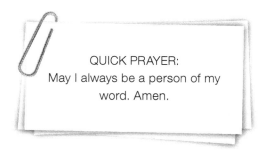

QUICK PRAYER:
May I always be a person of my
word. Amen.

JULY
21

Trustworthy

"At this, the administrators and the satraps tried to find grounds for charges against Daniel in his conduct of government affairs, but they were unable to do so. They could find no corruption in him, because he was trustworthy and neither corrupt nor negligent." (DAN 6:4)

Wow. If people were out to destroy us and had almost unlimited resources, could they find anything negligent about us? That is a very high standard. Daniel had been entrusted with enormous power and authority, yet no guile was found in him. His detractors could find no fault.

If we walk in a trustworthy manner, God will exalt us at work because He can trust us. The things that so easily ensnare and tempt us, when given no heed, become weak and loosen their hold.

When we walk in integrity, God is given opportunity to bless us because we are able to contain and channel greater blessing and influence without risking a large fall and disgrace.

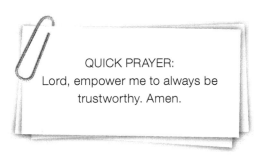

QUICK PRAYER:
Lord, empower me to always be
trustworthy. Amen.

JULY

22

You Are Allowed to Hate

"The righteous hate what is false, but the wicked make themselves a stench and bring shame on themselves." (Pro 13:5)

Hate sounds like such a negative emotion and largely that is true. Yet we are called to have a heart after God.

He experiences hate and anger and a righteous indignation, and so should we. It is Ok to hate what is false, to get angry about injustice and sin and the work of the enemy. We are encouraged to be angry yet not sin.

A walk with God in the workplace doesn't mean we become automatons, devoid of any emotion. We still are who we are. Sometimes we are frightened of our own emotive responses, as if they were purely fleshly and somewhat base. Yet Jesus wept, tossed people out of the temple, and often had a strong word to say to the religious that I am sure wasn't delivered in a dovelike monotone.

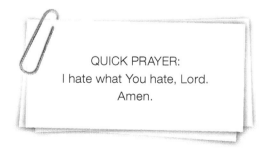

QUICK PRAYER:
I hate what You hate, Lord.
Amen.

JULY

23

Want to Shine?

"So that you may become blameless and pure, 'children of God without fault in a warped and crooked generation.' Then you will shine among them like stars in the sky." (Phi 2:15)

What does it take to shine in our generation? How do we become the example that stands out to those we employ or work with? How can we be a witness that shines a message clearly to those around us who are lost?

It is quite simple yet profound in its understatement and example. We shine by not living according to the prevailing standard but live in contrast to the society around us. We are commanded to be blameless and pure.

Can we do this is our own strength? No. We have to be reliant on Him who indwells us and can transform us. But as we live lives empowered by Him, we can be blameless and pure, and we will shine accordingly.

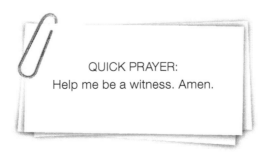

QUICK PRAYER:
Help me be a witness. Amen.

JULY
24

The Little Things

"Whoever can be trusted with very little can also be trusted with much, and whoever is dishonest with very little will also be dishonest with much." (LUK 16:10)

We are wired to consider the large things important and the small things inconsequential. As we go about our business days at work, we focus on the important and don't consider the mundane and small as important.

Yet in God's economy, He calls the small things to our attention as worthy of our focus. What we consider inconsequential, He says is important. God watches and sees how we handle the small things. He says that our attitude toward the little is the attitude we ultimately will have toward the large.

There is also a sense of promotion in this word where He will entrust us with more as we are faithful in the seemingly insignificant.

QUICK PRAYER:
Keep me faithful in the small
things, Lord. Amen.

Turning?

"Turn my heart toward your statutes and not toward selfish gain." (Psa 119:36)

What is important to us? By what standards do we live? If we are consumed by consumerism we will do anything to advance our agenda. If we are God fearing, we will be driven to follow His ways. Often we are somewhere in between, trying to balance our natural greed with the implementation of His way of doing things.

Ultimately our walk is governed by our relationship with Him. If we invest in spending time with God and fostering relationships, He will indwell our very hearts and empower us against our natural temptations to acquire and wander.

You can have success and gain without being selfish. It is not about what you have; it is about your heart and who you are.

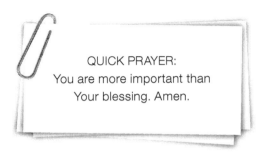

QUICK PRAYER:
You are more important than
Your blessing. Amen.

JULY

26

It Is Still True

"So in everything, do to others what you would have them do to you, for this sums up the Law and the Prophets." (Mat 7:12)

If there is one thing we could focus on that encompasses all it means to be a Christian, what would it be? What is the core of our behavior? It is the golden rule—not that he who has the gold make the rules but that we must treat others like we would like to be treated.

Are you in a management position? How do you like to be managed? Treat others like that. Who do you report to? How do you like those who report to you to work and relate? Often there is almost infinite wisdom in this simple yet revolutionary concept. Faithfully applied, this one principle will unlock limitless potential and fruit.

QUICK PRAYER:
"It is so simple yet so profound,
keep me focused on others,
Jesus." Amen.

Other Focus

"Not looking to your own interests but each of you to the interests of the others." (PHI 2:4)

Each of us is innately wired for self-preservation and self-fulfillment. There is actually nothing intrinsically flawed with that. It is how God has created us. However, we are called to look out for those around us. That is not to the denigration of our own interests but for the raising up of others so they are positioned as a priority.

We see what we focus on. Our attention is drawn to what is important to us. As we place priority on the interests of others, we will begin to see opportunities to meet needs and minister to those God has placed in our lives.

As we minister to those around us at work, we minister to Jesus.

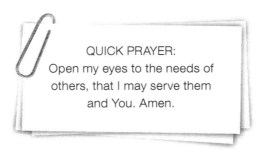

QUICK PRAYER:
Open my eyes to the needs of others, that I may serve them and You. Amen.

JULY

28

Where Do You Sit?

"I do not sit with the deceitful, nor do I associate with hypocrites." (Psa 26:4)

The church's—that's us, by the way—mission is to reach the lost. In order to do that, we have to be a part of their lives. Building a bastion on the hill and raising the drawbridge is not productive.

We should be mixing it up with all kinds of people and not just be isolated in a protective holy enclave. However, there is a closeness of relationship that comes with strong influences. We become like those we surround ourselves with. Making sure we are walking closely with people we respect is important. People who purport to have faith but don't live it and don't produce fruit in keeping with repentance should not be our closest confidants.

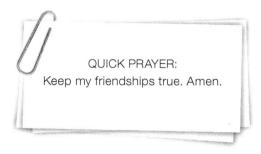

QUICK PRAYER:
Keep my friendships true. Amen.

JULY
29

Accounts

"And my honesty will testify for me in the future, whenever you check on the wages you have paid me. Any goat in my possession that is not speckled or spotted, or any lamb that is not dark-colored, will be considered stolen." (GEN 30:33)

Honesty is a foundational standard that testifies to our relationship with God. It is a 100 percent call to 100 percent honesty. Let us lay a standard that is beyond reproach regardless of who is checking us out.

I don't know about you, but I like to sleep at night. If we have confidence in doing a good job and being honest in all our declarations and actions, we can have confidence that we are beyond reproach.

If we are honest in the very small, seemingly insignificant things, we will be honest on the large things. Stay faithful and stay honest, and God will exalt you in due time.

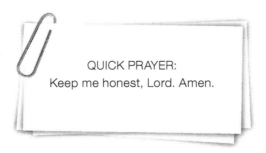

QUICK PRAYER:
Keep me honest, Lord. Amen.

JULY
30

Need Some Mercy?

"Whoever conceals their sins does not prosper, but the one who confesses and renounces them finds mercy." (Pro 28:13)

One of the down sides of an omnipotent God is that He sees everything. We have nowhere to hide. In fact, He knows what we are going to do even before we do it. Every dumb, crazy thing we will choose to do between now and when we die He is already fully aware of. We cannot surprise Him in any way.

So if we fall, let's not find a dark corner and have a pity party; let's not get into condemnation, saying, "God can never use me." Let's not stop meeting with Him as we wallow in our own disappointment and pride.

God has already forgiven you. He provided full pardon at the cross for all the sins of all men for all time. It is finished. Confess your sin, receive God's mercy, and move on.

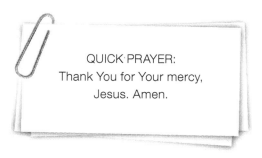

QUICK PRAYER:
Thank You for Your mercy,
Jesus. Amen.

Restitution

"Or whatever it was they swore falsely about. They must make restitution in full, add a fifth of the value to it and give it all to the owner on the day they present their guilt offering."
(Lev 6:5)

We are not subject to the law. We have been released from its hold and are free. However, the wisdom and precepts still come from the heart of God.

While we receive forgiveness for what we do wrong and Jesus has paid the price for that, there are often consequences for our actions. We need to look beyond our forgiveness and endeavor to make restitution to those we have offended or harmed.

Our forgiveness is not in question or reliant on any restitution we may make, but taking the time to heal wounds and put right wrongs is worthwhile.

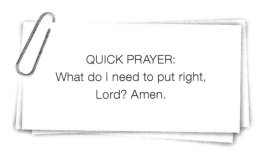

QUICK PRAYER:
What do I need to put right,
Lord? Amen.

AUGUST

1

Want to Know a Secret?

"For the Lord detests the perverse but takes the upright into his confidence." (PRO 3:32)

This is just one of those mind-blowing truths that is so large we miss it. The Creator of the universe would like to take you into His confidence. The only condition is uprightness. Now before you roll out a litany of things you have done wrong that exclude you, just wait.

You are justified by the blood of Jesus and have received His righteousness. Is Jesus upright? It is in His standing alone that we can hear from heaven, not by our own measure or works.

Take some time today to just wait on Him, read His Word, and wait. You may be astounded by what you hear.

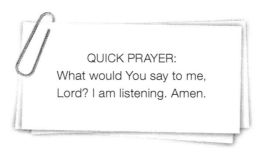

QUICK PRAYER:
What would You say to me,
Lord? I am listening. Amen.

You Are Secure

"Whoever walks in integrity walks securely, but whoever takes crooked paths will be found out." (PRO 10:9)

Worry is an odd emotion. It affects us all to one degree or another. Mostly it is irrational and is not a positive experience. Faith dispels fear, and as we realize how much God loves us and that He has a plan and a purpose to prosper us and not to harm us, we should be reassured.

So what do we need to do to secure what God has for us? When we walk with integrity, the Proverb tells us, we walk securely. Who would like to be secure? It would be a safe bet that all of us would consider security to be a positive.

Our integrity lays a path in line with God's will and therefore one that is straight and secure. In that truth we can have absolute confidence.

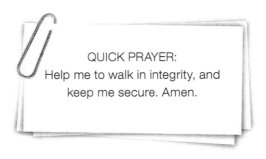

QUICK PRAYER:
Help me to walk in integrity, and
keep me secure. Amen.

AUGUST

3

Happiness

"His master replied, 'Well done, good and faithful servant! You have been faithful with a few things; I will put you in charge of many things. Come and share your master's happiness!'" (MAT 25:21)

Do you feel that what you have to do at work is less than you are capable of? Do you feel that you have more to give? The temptation under the circumstances is to treat what you have as somewhat unimportant.

The key to receiving more is being faithful with what you have. It is not to be done because you will get more but because we are asked to be faithful with what He has entrusted to us. Our faithfulness is rewarded by more responsibility and a share in our Master's happiness.

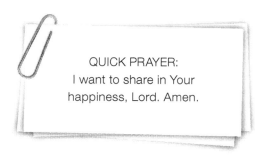

QUICK PRAYER:
I want to share in Your
happiness, Lord. Amen.

AUGUST
4

Treasure

"The house of the righteous contains great treasure, but the income of the wicked brings ruin." (PRO 15:6)

I can't say the word treasure without thinking of pirates. The paradox of that is that pirates are the antithesis of the righteous.

I am sure that the context of this treasure is blessing in its complete form. Peace, joy, provision, great relationships, health, and an open heaven—these are the things I would regard as treasure.

There is of course the obvious financial definition of treasure, and God is in the business of blessing us. Notice that it is the income of the wicked that brings the ruin. Both receive financially, but only one has treasure.

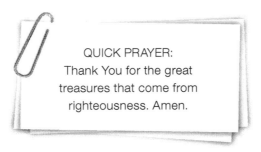

QUICK PRAYER:
Thank You for the great
treasures that come from
righteousness. Amen.

AUGUST
5

A Big Price to Pay

"Food gained by fraud tastes sweet, but one ends up with a mouth full of gravel." (PRO 20:17)

There is always a temptation to take the easy path. Often the easy answer has some inherent shortcuts or shortcomings. We can often justify this behavior by telling ourselves, "They will never know" or "It won't hurt anyone."

In the short term, it may even garner a good result. You may well get the quick win or the instant gratification. However, the Scripture here is very clear: in the longer term, there is always a price to pay for dishonesty or fraud.

Fraud doesn't have to be grand larceny; just some deception will be enough to meet the definition. A "mouth full of gravel" doesn't sound like an insignificant consequence ether. God's Word is to protect us, not to spoil the party.

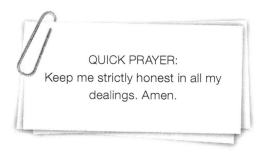

QUICK PRAYER:
Keep me strictly honest in all my dealings. Amen.

AUGUST
6

False Fortune

"A fortune made by a lying tongue is a fleeting vapor and a deadly snare." (Pro 21:6)

If you have accumulated some wealth, then how was it obtained? If it has been done with righteous labor and in acknowledgment that it comes from God, you can rest secure and enjoy what God has done for you.

On the other hand, if your fortune has been made and built on a foundation of deceit and dishonesty, it is merely a fleeting vapor. If this is your case, I would challenge you to make restitution and repent before God that He will have mercy.

Most of us in our fallen human state will have had times where we gained at the expense of others. We would do well to likewise ask for forgiveness and commit to working with complete honesty and integrity.

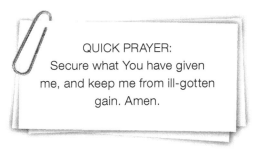

QUICK PRAYER:
Secure what You have given me, and keep me from ill-gotten gain. Amen.

AUGUST
7

Protector of the Poor

"Do not exploit the poor because they are poor and do not crush the needy in court." (Pro 22:22)

In our world, wherever we find ourselves, there will be those less fortunate than we are. If we live in a developed nation, we are merely by geographic location part of the privileged few.

We would be wise to consider the plight of those around us who do not have the advantages that we have. When we are in a position of authority or placed at some kind of hierarchical advantage, we must wait, think, empathize, and act with constraint. Don't take advantage just because you can. We have been forgiven much, and we are expected to act in kind.

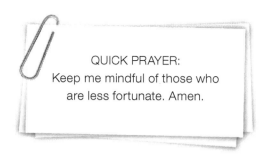

QUICK PRAYER:
Keep me mindful of those who
are less fortunate. Amen.

Greed

"The greedy bring ruin to their households, but the one who hates bribes will live." (Pro 15:27)

Our motivations feed our actions. If our main motivator is greed for material gain, we will eventually act on impulse to satisfy that motivation. Our greed is modified and balanced by a generous life when we are surrendered to the lordship of Christ.

When our motivation is to serve and honor Him, we will act in accordance with His will. When it comes to bribery, He has one standard and one alone. He hates bribery and encourages us to do likewise. The outcome of giving in to our own selfish desires is ruin. The outcome of leading a God-centered existence is life.

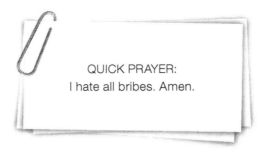

QUICK PRAYER:
I hate all bribes. Amen.

AUGUST

9

Blind Bribe

"Do not accept a bribe, for a bribe blinds those who see and twists the words of the innocent." (Exo 23:8)

There is no such thing as a small bribe, just as there is no such thing as a small lie. Satan is the father of all lies, so they come with a hook, usually in the form of an undesired or unexpected consequence.

The same is true for bribery. It can be as insidious as larger and larger bribes beginning to take hold in a life or community. The consequences described here in Exodus say that they blind those who see and twist the words of the innocent. What an accurate yet despicable depiction of truth being corrupted and purity being defiled.

It is important that we not only don't engage ourselves but that the practice is exposed in order to save those who would be the victims of its inevitable progression.

QUICK PRAYER:
Keep me from all bribes, subtle or obvious. Thank You, Lord.
Amen.

Work Works

"In the same way, faith by itself, if it is not accompanied by action, is dead." (JAM 2:17)

Our faith is important to us. It defines who we are and what we believe. Yet if it is not translated into actions, it is worthless, or as James, with his usual subtlety, puts it, dead.

This is as true at work as it is in church or in helping those who are less fortunate than ourselves. It is not only about giving; it is about being or even more correctly, about doing. There is no escaping this fundamental truth: our faith has to compel us into action if it is real. Without works, our faith is not real. A question for us all to consider is this: what do I do at work that demonstrates my faith?

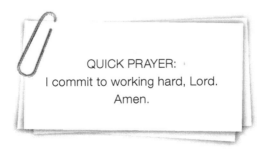

QUICK PRAYER:
I commit to working hard, Lord.
Amen.

AUGUST
11

What Shows the Love of God?

"If anyone has material possessions and sees a brother or sister in need but has no pity on them, how can the love of God be in that person?" (1 Joh 3:17)

How is the love of God demonstrated in us? What is the way in which our faith is demonstrated and evidenced? This powerful Scripture speaks to the reaction we have to those in need around us.

I had this verse printed on my checks. Back in the day before the proliferation electronic commerce, I used to write a lot of checks. It made me think about my priorities every time I wrote one out.

There are practical physical needs we can meet every day. Will we walk on by and have no pity, or will the love of God in us compel us to act?

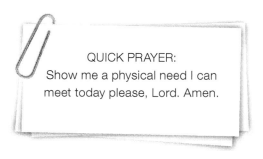

QUICK PRAYER:
Show me a physical need I can
meet today please, Lord. Amen.

Give in Love

"If I give all I possess to the poor and give over my body to hardship that I may boast, but do not have love, I gain nothing." (1 Cor 13:3)

What is our motivation to give? Giving is a good thing to do. We can give of our time and other resources, including, of course, financially. But why do we do it?

It could well be for a myriad of reasons. We may want to look successful. We may want others to see us as religious, spiritual, or generous. We may give out of guilt or to appease an image of a capricious God. We may give out of fear that if we don't, God will judge us or not bless us. There are so many false motivations, yet there is only one reason to give or to endure. It is the greatest of all motivations and the purest currency we have: love.

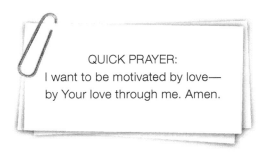

QUICK PRAYER:
I want to be motivated by love—
by Your love through me. Amen.

AUGUST
13

Happy to Give?

"Each of you should give what you have decided in your heart to give, not reluctantly or under compulsion, for God loves a cheerful giver." (2 Cor 9:7)

We are often told how to give and how much to give. God's way is clear, and it is not a formula. We should give as we have decided to give in our hearts. We are not to give reluctantly, nor should there be any measure of any kind of compulsory assumption.

How much are you happy to give? That sounds like an odd question, but it is worth considering. If God would like us to be cheerful when we give, how much are we happy to give cheerfully? Decide away from pressures and sermons in a quiet reflective time with God. Don't be reluctant, and do not feel forced in any way. Give out of a thankful heart in gratitude for all He has and will provide. Don't try to bribe God, and really, happily, cheerfully enjoy this wonderful act of worship.

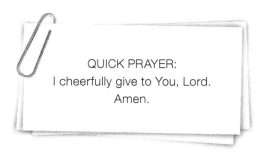

QUICK PRAYER:
I cheerfully give to You, Lord.
Amen.

AUGUST
14

Are You Moved?

"And everyone who was willing and whose heart moved them came and brought an offering to the Lord for the work on the tent of meeting, for all its service, and for the sacred garments." (Exo 35:21)

We are all part of the universal church of God. He has reflected His personality and various traits in a multitude of Christian expression in many denominations. We are here as His body to reach the lost with the truth.

Part of our responsibility is to fund the effective proclamation of the Gospel. That can take a multitude of expression, both locally and internationally and in so many wonderful ways.

We can be moved by personal gain or by the compassion of God to build His Kingdom. Giving to the work of God is one important way we can help be a part of the answer.

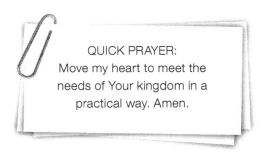

QUICK PRAYER:
Move my heart to meet the needs of Your kingdom in a practical way. Amen.

AUGUST

15

Giving as Worship

"On coming to the house, they saw the child with his mother Mary, and they bowed down and worshiped him. Then they opened their treasures and presented him with gifts of gold, frankincense and myrrh." (Mat 2:11)

When Jesus was a young child, the wise men came and worshipped Him. Then they gave Him gifts. This was a part of the act of paying homage to the newborn king. They honored Him with their giving.

We too are called to worship in our giving. Sometimes we can be moved to bring something of value to Him. It is not giving to a church or to a worthy cause but just giving something of value to Him, to worship and to adore.

I am not sure how that transaction occurs in our hearts, but it is certainly saying you are worth more to me than gold.

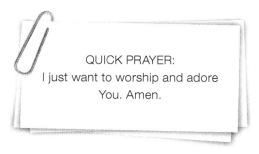

QUICK PRAYER:
I just want to worship and adore
You. Amen.

Sacrificial Giving?

"For I testify that they gave as much as they were able, and even beyond their ability. Entirely on their own." (2 Cor 8:3)

While we are all blessed with a brain and a certain amount of common sense, we sometimes have to be open to an unreasonable request. Giving in a practical sense meets the needs of the local church and other things we support. A measure of diligence and consistency is definitely required.

However, sometimes God will move our hearts in compassion for others. My strong recommendation is to go with your heart rather than your head. God will occasionally call you to give beyond all reason. His ways are not our ways, and sometimes it will be irrational from an earthly perspective.

When I have been moved in this way and been obedient to the call God, He has seen that it is put to good use. Often He will take what you have given and multiply its effect.

QUICK PRAYER:
"I know that sometimes you will call me to give beyond reason, keep me open to be obedient to your call." Amen.

AUGUST
17

What Is More Important?

"Woe to you, teachers of the law and Pharisees, you hypocrites! You give a tenth of your spices—mint, dill and cumin. But you have neglected the more important matters of the law— justice, mercy and faithfulness. You should have practiced the latter, without neglecting the former." (MAT 23:23)

There is a lot of chatter in churches about giving. If we were to be perfectly transparent with each other, it is usually by leaders who want you to give more and churchgoers looking to give less.

Is giving important? Yes it is, and it should not be neglected. But more important is justice, mercy, and faithfulness. These are the behaviors we should covet and endeavor to have in abundance.

Please give, and give regularly and generously, but never forget the priorities that are the fruit of a life transformed by Jesus: faithfulness, mercy, and justice.

QUICK PRAYER:
Thank You for the pattern and discipline of regular giving.
Amen.

How Can I Honor God?

"For where your treasure is, there your heart will be also."
(MAT 6:21)

We honor God by serving Him and being faithful to what He has called us to. Those of us in the marketplace have a responsibility to honor Him in all the arenas of life.

Our focus should always be on Him. Our focus is driven by our priorities, and our priorities are driven by our hearts. Our hearts will shape and mold our behaviors by what is truly important to us.

This Scripture says that our hearts, and therefore our motivations and behaviors, are driven by where our treasure is. What is our treasure? It obviously has financial implications, but I think it goes beyond just money. Our treasure is all that is important to us. If we invest time, relationships, and finances into the Kingdom of God, that is where our hearts will be.

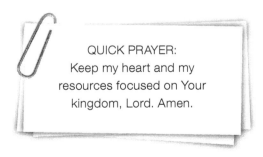

QUICK PRAYER:
Keep my heart and my resources focused on Your kingdom, Lord. Amen.

AUGUST

19

Casting

"Ship your grain across the sea; after many days you may receive a return." (Ecc 11:1)

I am quite simply the world's worst fisherman. It does not help matters that two of my brothers are experts. Going fishing with them is an exercise in futility and humility.

But one thing I do know is if you do not cast in your line, you will never catch a fish. Where you do not invest, it is absolutely certain you will never get a return. When you take no risk, you will not receive a reward. No sowing, no reaping.

We all know this, yet so often we are reluctant to take the risk. Many people in old age when talking about regret point to times they would have taken more risk, not less. So go on—go for it. Surround it in prayer, and "ship your grain across the sea." In due season, you will receive a return.

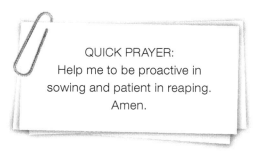

QUICK PRAYER:
Help me to be proactive in
sowing and patient in reaping.
Amen.

Rich in Many Ways

"You will be enriched in every way so that you can be generous on every occasion, and through us your generosity will result in thanksgiving to God." (2 Cor 9:11)

I love to give. This is something I can take no pride in. It is something God has done in my heart over many years. I have learned the joy of generosity as I have seen the fruit of sowing into people's lives.

God will ensure that we are enriched so we can be generous. What do you have in your hand? Is it just a little? Ask God to show you a need, and meet it. Joy will fill your heart, and He will be honored.

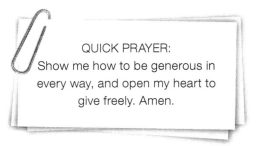

QUICK PRAYER:
Show me how to be generous in every way, and open my heart to give freely. Amen.

AUGUST

21

Giving and Hearing

"And said, 'Cornelius, God has heard your prayer and remembered your gifts to the poor." (ACT 10:31)

This almost sounds like an Old Testament Scripture. Surely our relationship with God is solely based on the forgiveness appropriated by Jesus? Yes, it is; you are quite correct. Yet just as we are forgiven in the measure we forgive others, so God sees our gifts to the poor and other acts and is moved and motivated by the evidence of a transformed heart.

When we are faithful, we are given more. We still reap what we sow even in this time of God's grace. There are consequences for actions, and He does still test our motivations and obedience. These are not popular concepts, but I have found them to still be true.

QUICK PRAYER:
Thank You that You listen to me
as I listen and act well toward
others. Amen.

AUGUST
22

Before the Law

"'And praise be to God Most High, who delivered your enemies into your hand.' Then Abram gave him a tenth of everything."
(GEN 14:20)

The truth of giving as a principle goes beyond the law. This example of giving predates Moses and the covenant. Abram (who would become Abraham) gave Melchizedek one-tenth of the spoils of war after a great victory.

We are not called the sons of Moses but the sons of Abraham, because we are children of faith, not children of the law. He is a model for us, as is his covenant, which is one of blessing and righteousness by faith. When God gives us victory and blessing, Abram showed us the way to give thanks and acknowledge who is our provider.

QUICK PRAYER:
Teach me about giving Your way—not man's way or a church's way but Your way; the way ordained for me. Amen.

AUGUST
23

Eating Your Tithe?

"Then exchange your tithe for silver, and take the silver with you and go to the place the Lord your God will choose. Use the silver to buy whatever you like: cattle, sheep, wine or other fermented drink, or anything you wish. Then you and your household shall eat there in the presence of the Lord your God and rejoice." (DEU 14:25–26)

Here is a Scripture that proponents of a legalistic approach to tithing may want to overlook. It says to take what you were going to give and go and buy wine, great food, and whatever else you want and have a great party before the Lord.

We have lost something of the heart of God if this makes us slightly uncomfortable. It makes me a bit uncomfortable. But why? It reflects the heart and desire of God to be joyful before Him, and He enjoys seeing us blessed. I think this is the kind of party where Jesus implored us to go to the highway and byways and invite the unlovely and socially unacceptable. Now that is what church is all about.

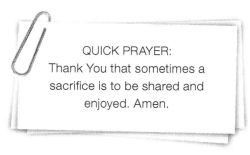

QUICK PRAYER:
Thank You that sometimes a sacrifice is to be shared and enjoyed. Amen.

Give to Provide

"So that the Levites (who have no allotment or inheritance of their own) and the foreigners, the fatherless and the widows who live in your towns may come and eat and be satisfied, and so that the Lord your God may bless you in all the work of your hands." (DEU 14:29)

Those of us who have been provided for have an obligation to meet the needs of others. In this case it is those who work fulltime for the church, foreigners, and those who have had misfortune in the loss of fathers and husbands, who were the providers of the time.

There are two groups that are a priority for God: those without finances and those who serve in church. We would do well to neglect neither.

There is a consequence attached to the actions we take. If we obey and provide for the poor and church workers, God Himself will bless us in all the work of our hands—that is, in our work at work.

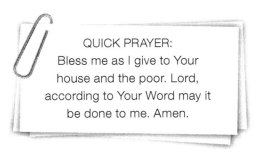

QUICK PRAYER:
Bless me as I give to Your house and the poor. Lord, according to Your Word may it be done to me. Amen.

AUGUST

25

Give as You Can

"According to their ability they gave to the treasury for this work 61,000 darics of gold, 5,000 minas of silver and 100 priestly garments." (Ezr 2:69)

The seemingly eternal question: how much should I give? If we have moved on from, "Should I give?" to the next stage, the question remains. We are called to give "according to our ability." Each one of us has been blessed in different ways and with different measure. We are to give according to our resources, yet we all have a part to play.

It is not the amount or even the proportion, but we are all able and willing to be a part of God's work and a reflection of His heart. Look at what God has already blessed you with. Decide in your thankful heart what to give, and give cheerfully according to your ability.

QUICK PRAYER:
Thank You that You ask me to give according to what You have already given me. Amen.

An Acceptable Gift

"For if the willingness is there, the gift is acceptable according to what one has, not according to what one does not have."
(2 COR 8:12)

When is a gift acceptable to God? It is an important question because there is no point in giving unless it is acceptable. Does the amount matter? No, God is interested in two things.

First, is it given willingly? When we give, it should be cheerfully and with a willing heart, not under duress or for selfish motives. Second, and I think somewhat surprisingly, it is to be given according to what one has.

It is not to be given in expectation of what we may receive or to be given according to what one does not have. We are called to give out of the harvest—out of the blessing we have already received.

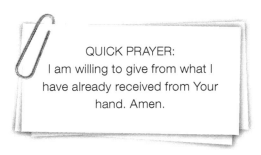

QUICK PRAYER:
I am willing to give from what I have already received from Your hand. Amen.

AUGUST

27

A Sacrifice

"But the king replied to Araunah, 'No, I insist on paying you for it. I will not sacrifice to the Lord my God burnt offerings that cost me nothing.' So David bought the threshing floor and the oxen and paid fifty shekels of silver for them." (2 Sam 24:24)

A sacrifice is not unsurprisingly meant to be a sacrifice. A sacrifice is nothing if it costs you nothing. A sacrifice is not an offering designed to appease a capricious deity. Our standing before God is unquestionable if we are washed in the blood of Jesus.

Yet sometimes it is good for us to give sacrificially to temper our own desires. Just as we train our bodies into a submitted state, we need to train our appetites and desires to keep them submitted to God.

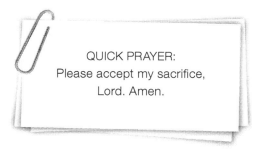

QUICK PRAYER:
Please accept my sacrifice,
Lord. Amen.

Give the Best

"Bring the best of the first fruits of your soil to the house of the Lord your God." (Exo 34:26)

When you bring a gift to a king, you would think twice before presenting something substandard. Just as we would honor an earthly king, so we should honor the King of Kings.

In this instance, not only are we asked to present the best but also that our offering should come from the first fruits. As God begins to bless us, we may need to consider how we can reserve the best for Him. That may take many forms depending on what the blessing may be. But one thing is for sure—only the best of the first fruits is appropriate to give. It also reminds us where the blessing has come from.

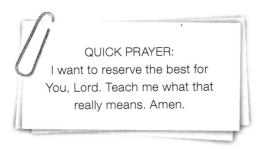

QUICK PRAYER:
I want to reserve the best for You, Lord. Teach me what that really means. Amen.

AUGUST
29

Are You Regular?

"On the first day of every week, each one of you should set aside a sum of money in keeping with your income, saving it up, so that when I come no collections will have to be made." (1 COR 16:2)

There are some universal and fundamental principles in life that are so simple that we almost take them for granted. If you want to save, save a little often and regularly, and you will save. If you want to have resources to give, put aside a regular amount every payday so you will get into the habit and establish a fund. Then when it is rime to give, you will be able to meet the needs or offer the gift.

Note also that this is in keeping with your income. If you earn a lot, put a large amount aside. If you are not earning much, put aside what you have determined in your heart before God to give. A little, put aside regularly, becomes significant quickly.

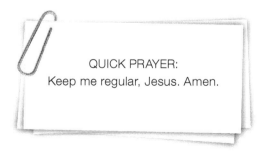

QUICK PRAYER:
Keep me regular, Jesus. Amen.

Complete Honesty

"They did not require an accounting from those to whom they gave the money to pay the workers, because they acted with complete honesty." (2 Kin 12:15)

Acting with honesty is often seen as a selfless act that is more about governing our own moral compass rather than any impact on others. However, when we act in a way that shows honesty and integrity, we create confidence in those who observe our behavior.

There is witness and testimony in complete honesty that results in respect and trust. When we demonstrate these characteristics, we will be given more responsibility and authority, as trust is a rare commodity.

Our reputations are built on the observation of our behavior, not in the motivations that produce them. Yet the behaviors can trigger the question of why we are acting in the way we do. That is the opportunity to share the foundation that underpins our faith.

QUICK PRAYER:
Build my reputation so that I am
held in complete trust, Lord.
Amen.

AUGUST

31

Family First

"Anyone who does not provide for their relatives, and especially for their own household, has denied the faith and is worse than an unbeliever." (1 Tim 5:8)

We have a responsibility for those around us. We are not isolated or insulated from the community into which God has positioned us. This is even more important when we consider our immediate family and relatives. How important does God consider our responsibility to provide for relatives? Could it really be more important than faith itself? Could that possibly be right? Read the Scripture in 1 Timothy 5:8 again.

There is not wriggle room in the Scripture. It is an outward sign that we are following Jesus. We have a God-given obligation to help our relatives and especially to provide for our immediate household.

I believe this responsibility goes beyond the financial and extends into the emotional, spiritual, and the all-important allocation of time and attention. That is a challenge to all of us with busy jobs and lives.

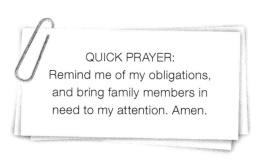

QUICK PRAYER:
Remind me of my obligations,
and bring family members in
need to my attention. Amen.

SEPTEMBER
1

Instructions for the Instructed

"Nevertheless, the one who receives instruction in the word should share all good things with their instructor." (GAL 6:6)

Whether we are at work or just life in general, there are always those around us that we glean wisdom from. They are usually older and have some good and bad life experience under their belts, although you can definitely learn from those younger as well. Regardless of the source of wisdom, we have a mandate to honor those who input into our lives.

If we receive instruction, then we are wise. So often we think we have all the answers, yet there is often another perspective we haven't seen. Honor mentors by listening and by sharing what is happening in your life. Those who are willing to provide wisdom usually have a good ear and an understanding heart.

QUICK PRAYER:
Lord, thank You for the mentors in my life. Remind me to say thanks and share what You are doing with me. Amen.

SEPTEMBER

2

Don't Be a Burden

"Surely you remember, brothers and sisters, our toil and hardship; we worked night and day in order not to be a burden to anyone while we preached the gospel of God to you." (1 The 2:9)

Not being a burden to those we are ministering to goes well beyond the financial support often required by ministers and missionaries. We can be a burden if we ask for other obligations to be met or are unusually demanding or fussy.

Being pleasant and easy to talk with and having a kind and peaceful demeanor are all evidence of the fruit of the Holy Spirit. They are in contrast to that which brings a burden.

Those we are ministering to are those we work with— our bosses and colleagues and those we lead. Does the measure of what it means to be a burden still apply in the workplace? Yes it does, as our job is our pulpit, and our workplace our mission field.

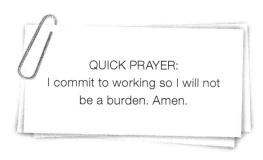

QUICK PRAYER:
I commit to working so I will not
be a burden. Amen.

Provision for the Vision

"And said to Moses, 'The people are bringing more than enough for doing the work the Lord commanded to be done.'" (Exo 36:5)

Something was right in the heart of the people under Moses. How many churches could say, "The people are bringing more than enough for doing the work the Lord commanded to be done."?

What would our world look like if all God was asking for us to give, in time, resources, attention, prayer, and finances, was being received into the kingdom of God? We would have a radically transformed world with an unheralded revival as we moved in unity with more than enough resources to fund the salvation of the world. If we do our part and encourage those around us to do the same, maybe we can start a revolution.

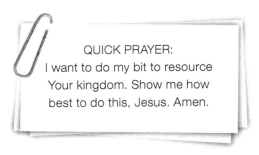

QUICK PRAYER:
I want to do my bit to resource Your kingdom. Show me how best to do this, Jesus. Amen.

SEPTEMBER
4

Asked

"Give to the one who asks you, and do not turn away from the one who wants to borrow from you." (MAT 5:42)

How are we asked to respond to those in need around us? What is our response to be to those who ask for help? Give and do not turn away. As we open our hands, we open our hearts. As we walk in obedience, we open our hearts and our hands follow suit. It is a virtuous cycle of love and giving.

If we live our lives this way, God will pour out His provision as He finds vessels willing to be His hands and His feet with His heart. Ministering to those around us is not only telling them about Jesus but also demonstrating His heart by meeting the needs of those who need help.

QUICK PRAYER:
I am available to bless someone today. Send me someone who needs help. Amen.

Is Your Brother in Need?

"Share with the Lord's people who are in need. Practice hospitality." (Rom 12:13)

They say that charity begins at home, and it is very true. We are a part of the family of God, born into His family as we accepted the Father's forgiveness and became sons and daughters of the King.

If we are now part of the family of God, we receive a multitude of promises and gifts that come with this honor and position. We also have responsibilities, just as we do in a natural family. We have a responsibility to help where we can, serve where we can, and give what we can.

We are called to share with the Lord's people and to practice hospitality. What a great and right thing to do.

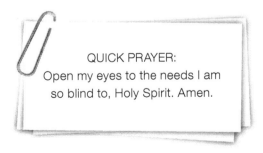

QUICK PRAYER:
Open my eyes to the needs I am
so blind to, Holy Spirit. Amen.

SEPTEMBER
6

Openhanded

"There will always be poor people in the land. Therefore I command you to be openhanded toward your fellow Israelites who are poor and needy in your land." (DEU 15:11)

I like words. I enjoy a word that perfectly describes what I am endeavoring to convey. Openhanded—what a wonderfully illustrative word that perfectly describes not only the physicality of a hand that gives but also a state of heart and even a lifestyle choice.

To live open handed is to live like Jesus—always ready to give, always ready to help, and always generous. Well, there is no other word for it—openhanded.

The opposite is just as demonstrable and also reflects not only the act but also the heart state behind the action: tight fisted. How would we best be described? Perhaps we are on the fence; maybe it is time to become more openhanded.

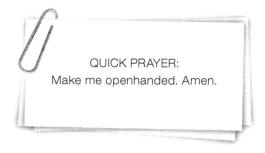

QUICK PRAYER:
Make me openhanded. Amen.

SEPTEMBER
7

How Many Do You Need?

"John answered, 'Anyone who has two shirts should share with the one who has none, and anyone who has food should do the same.'" (Luk 3:11)

How much is enough—one car, two cars, maybe three? How many pairs of pants can we wear? Do we need another toy? There are so many things I own that I didn't know I needed until I saw one. I have more things that Apple has made starting with an I than I would have ever thought possible a few years ago.

There is nothing wrong with material things or with owning nice products. The answer, I think, lies in their priority in our lives. Do we rate them above people? Do we not give to those in need because we want another toy?

I know of a businessman who drove an expensive Mercedes. One day he was driving along when he felt God was asking him to sell it and give the money away to a specific cause. He was obedient and now drives an even better car because God blessed him even more. Did he give to get? No, he gave in obedience and was subsequently blessed.

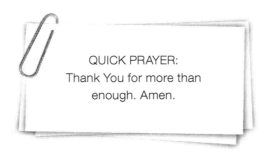

QUICK PRAYER:
Thank You for more than
enough. Amen.

SEPTEMBER

8

Hear My Cry

"Whoever shuts their ears to the cry of the poor will also cry out and not be answered." (PRO 21:13)

In our Western society, we are constantly bombarded with images on our TVs and computers of children in need, poverty, and untold distress in war, famine, and natural disasters. We have become inoculated to the truth that there are many in our world who are suffering terribly.

We have a litany of excuses. Some of my personal favorites are: What can I do? They have brought this on themselves. It is just another inefficient charity. They won't change. What is the point?

Fortunately God does not have the same heart as us. We will, however, be treated as we treat those who cry out for help, justice, and mercy.

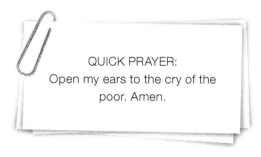

QUICK PRAYER:
Open my ears to the cry of the poor. Amen.

True Religion

"Religion that God our Father accepts as pure and faultless is this: to look after orphans and widows in their distress and to keep oneself from being polluted by the world." (Jam 1:27)

What is religion all about? Is it worship on a Sunday? Is it working hard? Is it letting others know about Jesus? All these things are true, but what does God say is the real heart, pure and faultless religion that He accepts as true?

First, there is a demonstration of an inward transformation: "to look after orphans and widows in their distress." Pure and simple, we have a significant God-given obligation to help the poor.

Second, we are called not to hide away from the world because this would make the first part impossible but to "keep oneself from being polluted by the world." Live in the world and fully participate, but don't take on its values and distortions.

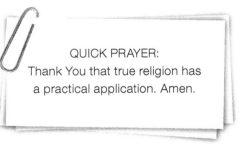

QUICK PRAYER:
Thank You that true religion has
a practical application. Amen.

SEPTEMBER
10

Giving or Reconciliation?

"Leave your gift there in front of the altar. First go and be reconciled to them; then come and offer your gift." (Mat 5:24)

At work we have ample opportunity to have disagreements, arguments, and conflict. What is our priority in God's view between making an offering to Him in giving or reconciliation with those we have crossed at work?

We are encouraged to first get our relationships straightened out and then come before God. Why is that? First, God is more into people than receiving an offering; they are much higher in His priorities. Second, He is more interested in our heart than our gift. When we seek restoration and reconciliation, we are moved to oppose pride, ego, and unhealthy attitudes. We are changed as we choose God's way over our way.

Third, when we come to God with a clear conscience, we are much more likely to commune with Him and receive in faith what He has for us.

QUICK PRAYER:
Bring to mind those with whom I need to be reconciled, and give me the strength and wisdom to act. Amen.

Better than Sacrifice?

"But Samuel replied: 'Does the Lord delight in burnt offerings and sacrifices as much as in obeying the Lord? To obey is better than sacrifice, and to heed is better than the fat of rams.'" (1 Sam 15:22)

What could be better that coming before God and offering praise and worship with gifts and offerings? Surely this is the pinnacle of our relationship with God and the ultimate expression of worship and faith.

Apparently not; God has a different view, and His opinion is that it is much more important to obey and to heed. We know what it means to obey, but the definition of heed gives us more insight: "to pay attention, to give consideration to, and to mind what someone says." It gives the sense of one listening with intent to act in obedience.

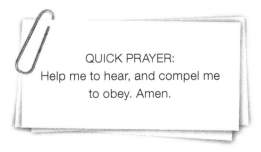

QUICK PRAYER:
Help me to hear, and compel me
to obey. Amen.

God Is a Worker

"By the seventh day God had finished the work he had been doing; so on the seventh day he rested from all his work." (GEN 2:2)

Is working an idea from God? Yes it is. He even demonstrated it from the beginning. We all know that He rested to demonstrate a day of rest, but He also worked to demonstrate work. It is blindingly obvious when you stop and think about it.

He planned, implemented, considered, and moved in structured steps. He stopped to review periodically, made sure it was good, and then moved to the next stage.

He could have spoken it all in one word, yet He chose to demonstrate work. Work is intrinsically good because it was birthed in the heart of God. It has value just in its execution. God is good, God works, and therefore work is good. What did He rest from? Work.

QUICK PRAYER:
Thank You for demonstrating work and showing that it has value. Amen.

SEPTEMBER 13

Jesus Is a Worker

"In his defense Jesus said to them, 'My Father is always at his work to this very day, and I too am working.'" (JOH 5:17)

Work is ordained in the heavenlies. What you do at work is good because God has asked you to do it. Companies that exist to honor God do so regardless of the output or the other things they fund; they have a right to exist in God's economy because work is ordained on high.

Jesus worked for many years before His public ministry. Did He honor God during that time? How good were the products He produced as a carpenter? Was He pleasing His Father while at work? Surely these are rhetorical questions.

Jesus described His public ministry as work and even said that the Father is always at work. He is not a stranger to our workday experience and has a plan and purpose for your every day.

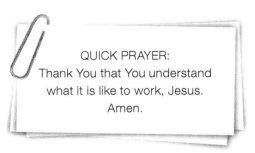

QUICK PRAYER:
Thank You that You understand
what it is like to work, Jesus.
Amen.

SEPTEMBER
14

A Divine Order

"Six days you shall labor and do all your work." (Exo 20:9)

Are we called to labor? Are we called to work? This Scripture is often quoted as a pointer to the importance of Sabbath, and quite rightly so. But how often do we give ascendency and importance to the rest while ignoring the God-given instruction to labor and call to work?

Without labor there is no rest. God instructs us to work, and God instructs us to rest. There is a balance and restoration in recognizing a calling to both. Both honor God, both bring blessing, and both should be acknowledged as God's provision and will.

If we labor well and according to God's principles, we will bring blessing to ourselves, our family, and those around us. If we honor the Sabbath, we will be refreshed and balanced in our relationships with God, family, and community. If we honor and obey God's instructions to rest, we are then available to do His will for the other six days.

QUICK PRAYER:
I didn't think I would say this, but
thank You for work. Amen.

Be Useful

"Anyone who has been stealing must steal no longer, but must work, doing something useful with their own hands, that they may have something to share with those in need." (EPH 4:28)

Work is ordained by God and categorized by Him as useful. Here it is evidenced by a change in behavior from destructive to constructive. This indicates that work is not only useful but also purposeful. The purposeful characteristic demonstrated is the act of giving.

There are many positive outcomes of working. If we take a look at those who are not working, we can see the destructive nature of long-term unemployment, often through no fault of their own.

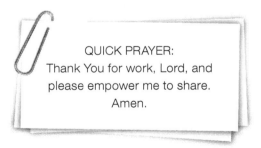

QUICK PRAYER:
Thank You for work, Lord, and
please empower me to share.
Amen.

SEPTEMBER
16

Expectation

"Then people go out to their work, to their labor until evening."
(Psa 104:23)

We sometimes complain about work and the stress and tiredness it can produce. Yet there is something very fulfilling about a good day's work. When we know that we have worked hard and got a good result, it can be very rewarding and satisfying.

Whether you work physically or at a desk, regardless of your role, you can rest easy and well with a full day's work.

I have seen people motivated by a special project to the extent they don't want to stop. It can be a very rewarding day when we have given all to a common cause. It is God's expectation that we commit to our work and do it all with excellence. The outcome for us is satisfaction and the reward of knowledge we are working for Him.

QUICK PRAYER:
A full day's work is a good and
satisfying endeavor. Amen.

What Do You Do?

"Amos answered Amaziah, 'I was neither a prophet nor the son of a prophet, but I was a shepherd, and I also took care of sycamore-fig trees.'" (Amo 7:14)

When we go to a party or meet strangers in a networking event, we are often asked the question, "What do you do?" We can identify with what we do, and there is nothing really wrong with that.

What about if we were in a room full of fulltime church workers? Maybe there are many missionaries, pastors, priests, and social and charity workers there. How would we feel about our profession then? Would we place our vocation on some kind of spiritual pecking order?

The truth is that God has called us each to play a role in His kingdom. You have a sacred calling to do what you do. There is no hierarchy of callings; each is anointed, appointed, and placed in a specific role for a definitive, God-ordained purpose.

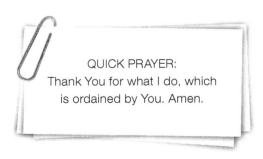

QUICK PRAYER:
Thank You for what I do, which
is ordained by You. Amen.

SEPTEMBER
18

Promotion

"So Pharaoh said to Joseph, 'I hereby put you in charge of the whole land of Egypt.'" (GEN 41:41)

There is a payday for those who follow God and work in His way. Joseph was gifted by God and disciplined and diligent in his execution of God's purposes. He had a hard road to walk but then had the ultimate promotion.

He followed God's ways and had God's insights and wisdom. He moved well in the supernatural and in the natural. He is an example for us. It is God who exalts and God who promotes. He is interested in us fulfilling our potential. If we walk His way and work His way, we will ultimately fulfill our true calling and unlock our full potential.

QUICK PRAYER:
You are the promoter and exalter; I surrender to You, Your timing, and Your way. Amen.

Structure

"It pleased Darius to appoint 120 satraps to rule throughout the kingdom, with three administrators over them, one of whom was Daniel. The satraps were made accountable to them so that the king might not suffer loss." (Dan 6:1–2)

There is one law of leadership that many entrepreneurs never quite master. If you do not clearly structure by responsibility and empower those people to make decisions, you will not grow your business.

When we are given any level of responsibility, fulfilling it with diligence does not mean doing it all ourselves. Leveraging team relationships and structuring authority coupled with clear objectives, division of responsibility, clear, demonstrable goals, and the articulation of an inclusive vision will all lead to success.

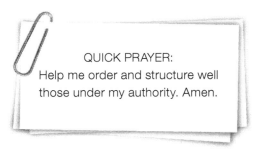

QUICK PRAYER:
Help me order and structure well
those under my authority. Amen.

SEPTEMBER
20

Influence

"So he started out, and on his way he met an Ethiopian eunuch, an important official in charge of all the treasury of the. This man had gone to Jerusalem to worship." (ACT 8:27)

Phillip was told to go and wait on a specific road. Had he not been listening to God, he would not have been there. God placed him there for a specific purpose. He then had the courage to abandon protocol and talk to an important person about Jesus. Philip would explain to a seeker what the Bible meant and who Jesus was.

The influence Phillip had over the Ethiopian eunuch not only led to the salvation of an important man, but it also led to the birth of a Christian nation in Africa. A whole country and then millions on a new continent were influenced by one man being obedient to the prompting of God.

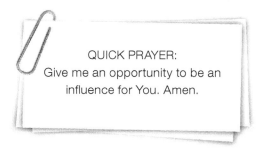

QUICK PRAYER:
Give me an opportunity to be an
influence for You. Amen.

SEPTEMBER
21

Even a Rag Trader?

"One of those listening was a woman from the city of Thyatira named Lydia, a dealer in purple cloth. She was a worshiper of God. The Lord opened her heart to respond to Paul's message." (ACT 16:14)

I cut my teeth in the textile industry in its many forms. Having spent so much time in this commercial arena, it is good to see that God even calls 'rag traders' into the kingdom. He is obviously no respecter of persons or professions, yet the Scripture clearly identifies Lydia with her profession.

Lydia was a dealer is purple cloth and a very successful businesswoman. She came to hear what Paul had to say. It says she was a worshiper of God. When we seek after Him, He will respond. God then worked on her heart to give her revelation.

Lydia remained in business and was a successful person serving God in that capacity, having received a full revelation of Jesus.

QUICK PRAYER:
Thank You that You call us from
all professions and identify us by
what we do. Amen.

SEPTEMBER

22

Authority

"Slaves, obey your earthly masters with respect and fear, and with sincerity of heart, just as you would obey Christ." (Eph 6:5)

Who do you work for? We all have bosses, boards, shareholders, managers, or others in authority over us. Regardless of our role, we are all responsible to someone.

Some of us may have unreasonable, over-demanding, or overbearing people in authority over us; others are kind, responsible, and approachable leadership. Regardless of who our oversight is or how they operate, we have a clear guideline as to how to treat them: with respect and sincerity. That is not easy in our sometimes-tough commercial existence. How can we do that with genuine sincerity and true respect?

The key for me is the motivation of our hearts. We are to treat those in authority over us as we would treat Jesus. Would we be motivated, loyal, trustworthy, honest, hardworking, excellent, and go the extra mile for our living Savior? Then we are to treat those He puts in authority over us in the same way.

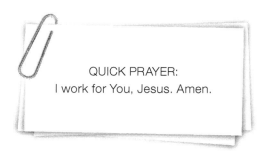

QUICK PRAYER:
I work for You, Jesus. Amen.

God's Workmanship

"For we are God's handiwork, created in Christ Jesus to do good works, which God prepared in advance for us to do."
(EPH 2:10)

What on earth are You doing, God? These words are all to frequent in my prayers and I am sure in yours as well. Often we do not see the purpose, reason, or plan God is enacting in our lives. Sometimes, even often, we will just not understand why things are happening.

We just have to trust that God knows what He is doing. Have you given your life to Him? Then He is at liberty to do whatever He wants. We are His workmanship and His handiwork, designed by Him for His purposes.

The outcome as we surrender to His will in faith is good works and not just manmade good ideas. God made good works prepared by Him before we were even created.

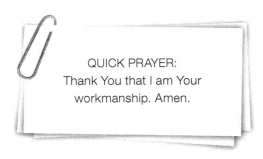

QUICK PRAYER:
Thank You that I am Your
workmanship. Amen.

SEPTEMBER
24

Builders

"Unless the Lord builds the house, the builders labor in vain. Unless the Lord watches over the city, the guards stand watch in vain." (Psa 127:1)

There are many ways you can approach a problem, opportunity, or project, but when you boil it all down, there are only really two: your way or God's way. There is a war in our flesh between the pull of the old nature, independent, proud, and rebellious, and the new nature, anointed and motivated by God.

If we proceed in our own strength, then we alone are responsible for the outcome, and God has to stay on the sidelines. If we do it His way, then He will build a strong foundation, bring lasting fruit, and protect what is His.

At the end of your life, all you did in your own strength will be burned up and all you did in God's plan in His way will go with you into eternity. Now that's worth thinking about.

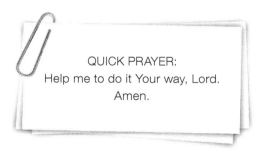

QUICK PRAYER:
Help me to do it Your way, Lord.
Amen.

Disorder

"For where you have envy and selfish ambition, there you find disorder and every evil practice." (Jam 3:16)

How is your life at work going? Is there discord and disorder and lots of undesirable stuff happening? Maybe this is happening in other parts of your life. While we can always point the finger at others, we can do little to impact their motivation, save for the acceptance of the Gospel.

What we can do is to look into our own hearts and see if there is anything in us that needs to be yielded to God. This Scripture says that the outcomes of envy and selfish ambition are discord and evil practices.

We are called not to envy, which is oh so easy to do. Selfish ambition can be very easily dressed up in the respectability of wanting influence or leadership or provision for our families. Ask the Holy Spirit to examine your heart and straighten out your motivations; I will be.

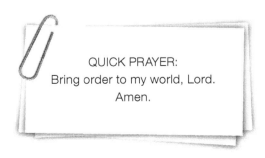

QUICK PRAYER:
Bring order to my world, Lord.
Amen.

SEPTEMBER
26

Have a Crack!

"Have I not commanded you? Be strong and courageous. Do not be afraid; do not be discouraged, for the Lord your God will be with you wherever you go." (Jos 1:9)

Have a crack! Give it a go! Just do it! Don't hold back! If you have been sitting on that great idea, stop hatching it out and go and put it into practice. A very successful businessman once told me that the only difference between him and a lot of other less successful people was that he "had a crack."

Everyone has good ideas or says the all too familiar, "Someone should..." The difference between most of us and the successful few is that the few put it onto practice, take the risk, jump out, and start something.

We are the strong and courageous ones with God on our side, and He will be with us wherever we go. So today just be strong and courageous.

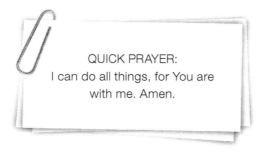

QUICK PRAYER:
I can do all things, for You are
with me. Amen.

It Will Come

"But as for you, be strong and do not give up, for your work will be rewarded." (2 CHR 15:7)

Hope delayed makes the heart sick. I know what it is like to be waiting and waiting and trying to do the right thing and seeing no result; nothing, just a seemingly empty void with no answer from God. In these times, we begin to question so many things.

But wait—stop and wait. Be strong, and do not give up! So many have fallen at the last hurdle just before the dawn, to combine and mangle a couple of metaphors.

Again, be strong and do not give up; your work will be rewarded. Your reward is coming. Hear it again: your work will be rewarded. God sees what you are doing, He has not abandoned you and is faithful in fulfilling His promises.

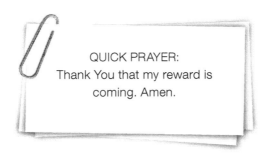

QUICK PRAYER:
Thank You that my reward is
coming. Amen.

SEPTEMBER
28

Discouraging People

"Then the peoples around them set out to discourage the people of Judah and make them afraid to go on building." (Ezr 4:4)

When we step out to be obedient to the call of God, one thing is certain. We will get opposition. If you are walking the way of God, you will get flack from the strangest of places.

One of the favorite ways the enemy seeks to oppose us is through discouragement. You will never get that done. Who are you to do that? That's too big a dream. You must be joking. That will never work. All that is just within your own head; just wait until others start talking to you.

Be prepared, and expect discouragement from others. Recognize it for what it is, respond gracefully, and set your face like flint. Strengthen those feeble knees, lean into the wind, and go forward regardless of the opposition.

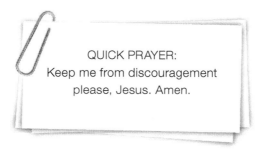

QUICK PRAYER:
Keep me from discouragement
please, Jesus. Amen.

SEPTEMBER
29

Keep Going

"So we continued the work with half the men holding spears, from the first light of dawn till the stars came out." (NEH 4:21)

What is our response when we get opposition? You may be making changes at work that are not being received well. How do we build what God intends and still protect ourselves? Sometimes we just have to persevere.

When Nehemiah was rebuilding the walls of Jerusalem and got opposition, he did two things. First, he put in place a strategy to protect what he was doing and the people who were building. Second, he doubled his efforts and pushed harder to get the job done. Opposition did garner a response and a strategy, but the result was a more determined and motivated workforce eager to get the work of God completed.

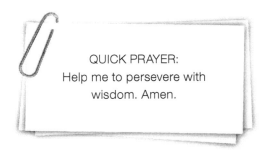

QUICK PRAYER:
Help me to persevere with wisdom. Amen.

SEPTEMBER

30

Go Hard

"Whatever your hand finds to do, do it with all your might, for in the realm of the dead, where you are going, there is neither working nor planning nor knowledge nor wisdom." (Ecc 9:10)

We only pass by this world once. We are not reincarnated, remade, or recycled. It is appointed to men to live once, and then comes judgment. This day, when it is gone, cannot be redeemed, and it is one less day you are here on the earth.

How then should we respond to this truth? How should it make us live? How does this self-evident truth affect us and how we should approach our work?

In Ecclesiastes it says we should work with all our might; these are strong words but not unreasonable when you look from an eternal perspective. So whatever your hand finds to do today, do it with all you've got, because you won't be here in this moment again.

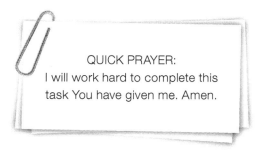

QUICK PRAYER:
I will work hard to complete this
task You have given me. Amen.

Try a Few Things

"Sow your seed in the morning, and at evening let your hands not be idle, for you do not know which will succeed, whether this or that, or whether both will do equally well." (Ecc 11:6)

I am a big believer in focus. Focused energy and resources will ensure an outcome when applied to a task. However, a diversified portfolio is wise because having all your eggs in one basket contains focused risk.

The same principle applies to what we work on. Some things will work and others just won't, so trying a number of ventures is not unwise.

The other imperative in this word is that of application. You can't get away from plain old hard work. A number of different projects require more effort. It is not about diluting your resources; it is about increasing your opportunities. And who knows—maybe it will all be successful.

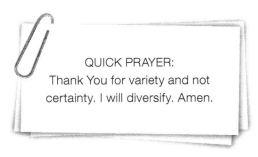

QUICK PRAYER:
Thank You for variety and not certainty. I will diversify. Amen.

OCTOBER

2

Passion

"So we rebuilt the wall till all of it reached half its height, for the people worked with all their heart." (Neh 4:6)

I love being around passionate people. There is something right and good and empowering in being surrounded by people who are motivated, engaged, and passionate about what they are doing at work.

These people believe in what they are doing, understand their part in it, and have a heart for the outcome and the journey. Their motivation tends to be external rather than a selfish ambition. The vision is more important than their personal desires. They have sacrificed to be a part of something bigger.

As followers of Christ, we are part of the salvation plan for mankind. Could there be any bigger cause? Could there be any greater task? If you have lost some passion, ask God to ignite it afresh and people will be drawn to you.

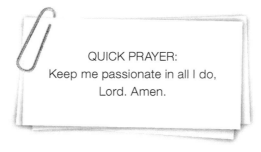

QUICK PRAYER:
Keep me passionate in all I do,
Lord. Amen.

OCTOBER
3

Reward Hard Work

"The hardworking farmer should be the first to receive a share of the crops." (2 TIM 2:6)

Are you in a position of authority? Has God given you the honor of leadership? We all have areas of our work where we are given a position of responsibility or where we rely on or influence others. It is very rare that an individual is completely self-reliant for an outcome.

Whether we are in a direct leadership role or not, we should reward those who work hard on our behalf. Whether that reward is a token of thanks or payment for productivity is not important. It is the honoring of the hard work that pays true dividends.

Company productivity is enhanced when those who work hard are disproportionately rewarded. Our egalitarian culture is fine in many respects, but rewards for hard work and productivity should be a direct correlation.

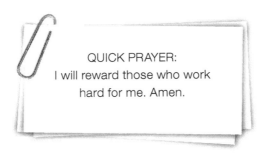

QUICK PRAYER:
I will reward those who work
hard for me. Amen.

OCTOBER
4

Results

"Those who work their land will have abundant food, but those who chase fantasies have no sense." (PRO 12:11)

There is always something enticing about the latest idea, the new venture that is still shiny in its new box. We can spend a lot of time on the new when the slightly old has lost its shine.

There is a time to explore new opportunities, and there is a time for good, old-fashioned, hard graft where we knuckle down and work hard on what we already have.

In its extreme, the entrepreneurial spirit can be distracted by the next idea while the last one dies on the shelf for lack of focus and resources. Sometimes we need to complete the last venture and not start a new thing.

QUICK PRAYER:
Keep me focused on the task at hand please, Holy Spirit. Amen.

Protect It

"The one who guards a fig tree will eat its fruit, and whoever protects their master will be honored." (PRO 27:18)

When we are given responsibility at work we need to receive it with a sense of responsibility. If we treat it well as if it were our own it will bear fruit.

When we protect the areas we are given with integrity and excellence, they will prosper. The byproduct of this is that we will actually be blessed by what we protect. He who guards the tree will eat of its fruit.

Plus, as we operate in a spirit of protection we will be given more responsibility because we will be deemed trustworthy by God and man.

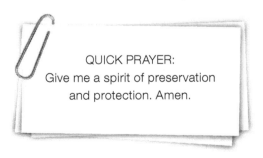

QUICK PRAYER:
Give me a spirit of preservation
and protection. Amen.

OCTOBER
6

Little by Little

"Dishonest money dwindles away, but whoever gathers money little by little makes it grow." (Pro 13:11)

Those get rich quick schemes draw people in because the desire to get wealth outweighs their common sense of testing an opportunity. The old saying is that if it looks too good to be true, then it probably is.

If we take shortcuts in how we earn, whether that is in overcharging, having an inferior product, dodging taxes, or not paying our creditors, God will not honor our income. It becomes fleeting and fragile, built on an unsure foundation.

When we do it right, earn an honest income, and invest wisely, it may seem to be little by little, but you will build a solid foundation that God will look at and cause to grow.

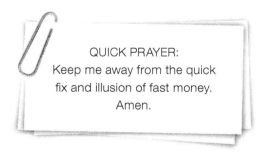

QUICK PRAYER:
Keep me away from the quick
fix and illusion of fast money.
Amen.

Get It In

"He who gathers crops in summer is a prudent son, but he who sleeps during harvest is a disgraceful son." (Pro 10:5)

There is wisdom in understanding the season you are in. There is a time to reap and a time to sow; other times are winter, where nothing seems to happen and patience is required.

The responsibility we have in summer is to reap the harvest. We can be in different seasons in different areas of our lives at the same time. Discerning what season we are in is important. There is no point in sowing in winter.

There are financial harvests, spiritual harvests, and even relationship harvests. What season are you in now, and what area is ready for harvest? We have to be diligent and aware, for the season of harvest is short and temporary.

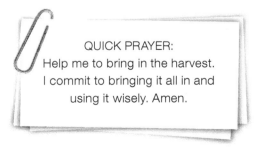

QUICK PRAYER:
Help me to bring in the harvest.
I commit to bringing it all in and
using it wisely. Amen.

OCTOBER

8

What Makes You Poor?

"Lazy hands make for poverty, but diligent hands bring wealth." (Pro 10:4)

We are often quick to blame God for all our problems. Other people and circumstances are reasonable targets as well. It is always easier to look elsewhere when blame is to be apportioned.

This is not about a guilt trip, and I certainly wouldn't want to place any condemnation on you, but when we do not apply ourselves to the tasks assigned to us, there are consequences that are real and physical, including missing a promotion or being disciplined at work.

The Bible says lazy hands lead to poverty, yet the hope is that He is always ready to help you with a turnaround. The outcome He wants is for you to be blessed, and diligent hands bring wealth.

QUICK PRAYER:
I'm sorry for when I slack off.
Help me to work well and wisely.
Amen.

OCTOBER
9

Talker?

"All hard work brings a profit, but mere talk leads only to poverty." (Pro 14:23)

I have plenty of things I am going to get around to. If I talk about them for years, they still won't get done. It is only when we stop talking and start doing that we make progress.

Our words have to translate into action to be effective. If you want to talk about the latest idea, project, business model, or whatever, put timeframes into the discussion. This can help you crystalize a plan and start to progress to action.

It is a lot easier to talk than to work. It is the easier option. It is hard work that brings a profitable result. Talk without action leads only to more talk and no outcome.

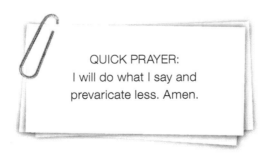

QUICK PRAYER:
I will do what I say and
prevaricate less. Amen.

OCTOBER
10

Skill

"Tell all the skilled workers to whom I have given wisdom in such matters that they are to make garments for Aaron, for his consecration, so he may serve me as priest." (Exo 28:3)

We have all been built for a purpose. Part of that is our unique set of skills, temperament, and physical attributes. The skills need to be grown, nurtured, and developed, but their origin is a gift from God.

Those skills are for an outcome and a specific purpose. He has handcrafted you for a mission. Most of us will see that in a so-called secular job. He has equipped us to be effective in what He has called us to do. Your job is a specific calling from your Creator to use the skill set He built you with. You can serve Him as you serve others and as your skill set is used productively in the commercial sector.

Offering our skills to God and acknowledging they come from Him takes us to another level where is anointing can sharpen, hone, and enlarge are skills to make us even more effective in His hands.

QUICK PRAYER:
Bless the skills You have given
me to fulfill my purpose in You.
Amen.

A Gift of Wisdom

"Therefore wisdom and knowledge will be given you. And I will also give you wealth, possessions and honor, such as no king who was before you ever had and none after you will have." (2 Chr 1:12)

Solomon made a wise choice when he asked God for wisdom and knowledge. God gave them to Solomon in abundance and then loaded him down with wealth, possessions, and honor. While these were additional gifts and ultimately had their origin in God, I believe they were an outcome of the application of the initial gifts.

When we ask for wisdom and knowledge in an area of our lives, He will give us what we need. When we take that wisdom and knowledge and actually put our hand to the plough and apply what we have received, then and only then do we reap a physical harvest.

QUICK PRAYER:
Thank You for the myriad of gifts You have given me. Help me to work in the anointing You have blessed me with. Amen.

OCTOBER

12

A Gift of Knowledge

"He changes times and seasons; he deposes kings and raises up others. He gives wisdom to the wise and knowledge to the discerning." (DAN 2:21)

You would think giving wisdom to the wise would be a bit redundant. If they are wise, why would you give them more wisdom? In God's economy, the last shall be first and those who have will be given more. The faithful receive, and those who give away receive more.

Hearing from God and discerning the seasons brings knowledge and understanding as well as insight and advantage. Seeing what is in ascendency and what is slowing down is a good skill to have in business. If we can discern trends and moves, we can position a company to take full advantage of a soon-coming harvest.

QUICK PRAYER:
You ordain seasons. Help me
to discern them and operate
accordingly. Amen.

Success

"When his master saw that the Lord was with him and that the Lord gave him success in everything he did." (GEN 39:3)

Sometimes we can become so spiritual that we are no earthly good. Walking with Jesus under the blessing of God has very real consequences for the here and now as well as the hereafter.

The practical application of Godly principles under the unction and anointing of God will bring success. It may not come in the form you expect, and the road may well be difficult, but you will be successful.

God can give you success in everything you do. That is just as important in a work and business context as it is in relationships and church work.

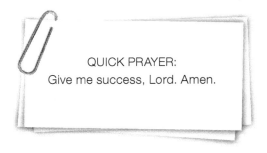

QUICK PRAYER:
Give me success, Lord. Amen.

OCTOBER

14

Repayment

"May the Lord repay you for what you have done. May you be richly rewarded by the Lord, the God of Israel, under whose wings you have come to take refuge." (Rut 2:12)

God is no man's debtor. He sees what we do and rewards us. While what we do has no bearing on our salvation, we still reap what we sow. We do not appease Him by works, but we work out of a grateful heart for what He has already accomplished on our behalf.

There are seasons where you wonder what is going on. Where is the deliverance you have prayed for? Where is the answer to that prayer you have prayed for so long? Where is the breakthrough you have longed for?

Worrying, striving, arguing, or trying to convince God will just wear you out. Notice that the reward is given for what you have done, but the position you have is resting under His wings.

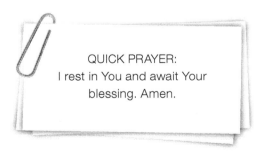

QUICK PRAYER:
I rest in You and await Your
blessing. Amen.

OCTOBER
15

A Gracious Hand

"I also told them about the gracious hand of my God on me and what the king had said to me. They replied, 'Let us start rebuilding.' So they began this good work." (NEH 2:18)

The hand of God is gracious. That is a beautiful picture of how He influences us with His grace—a loving heavenly Father reaching down and gracefully touching and moving our hearts, spirits, and minds.

When the hand of grace is on you, the hearts of kings can be moved on your behalf. The favor of the people around you can materialize. The purpose of His grace, the moving of hearts, and the favor of the people was to complete a good work.

God always has a purpose when He intervenes in our affairs. He is an active participant in our lives and has good works for us to do that are prepared before the beginning of time.

QUICK PRAYER:
Thank You for Your gracious
hand. Amen.

OCTOBER

16

A Good Frustration

"When our enemies heard that we were aware of their plot and that God had frustrated it, we all returned to the wall, each to our own work." (NEH 4:15)

Whether we choose to acknowledge it or not, we are in a war for souls. When we are at work or at home, we have a very real enemy who will oppose us whenever He can. Thank God that He holds back the full fury of the enemy.

If the world were to see the fullness of evil that has blinded them or the consequences of going into a Christless eternity, they would run into the hands of our loving Savior.

God is able to protect us and frustrate the plans of the evil one. He frustrates the devil's schemes and makes us aware of what is happening in the spiritual.

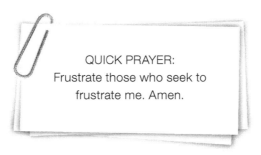

QUICK PRAYER:
Frustrate those who seek to
frustrate me. Amen.

What Can You Receive?

"To this John replied, 'A person can receive only what is given them from heaven.'" (JOH 3:27)

All we have and all we are comes from the hand of the Father. All we achieve and receive comes from heaven. No one can boast and say that they have achieved this and that, for without God we would have nothing.

A gift can only be of value to a person who is willing to receive it. What is the position of our heart when it comes to receiving His gifts at work? If we assume that we are to operate in our own strength at work and that God is not really interested, there is a consequence. There will be gifts He has to give us that we do not receive because our hearts and prayers are not positioned to receive.

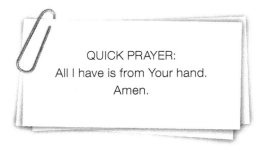

QUICK PRAYER:
All I have is from Your hand.
Amen.

OCTOBER

18

Up and Down

"It is God who judges: He brings one down, he exalts another."
(Psa 75:7)

If you are looking to be promoted or exalted in some way or another, take a look at this Scripture. First the question is why? While it is true that if we wait for pure motivation, we will all be waiting a long time, God is quite clearly not into selfish ambition.

He is, however, into blessing people and placing His faithful ones into positions of influence and authority where He can impact the world with His love and see His Kingdom expanded.

The down side of acknowledging that God is in the business of exalting people is that He is also in the habit of repositioning people in the other direction. Why on earth would He do that to someone on His team? Perhaps we need some measure of humility, more time with family, or some other reason we can't even fathom. But one thing is for sure: He is not capricious, and He always has our best in mind.

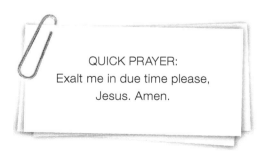

QUICK PRAYER:
Exalt me in due time please,
Jesus. Amen.

OCTOBER
19

Stirred Up

"So the Lord stirred up the spirit of Zerubbabel son of Shealtiel, governor of Judah, and the spirit of Joshua son of Jozadak, the high priest, and the spirit of the whole remnant of the people. They came and began to work on the house of the Lord Almighty, their God." (HAG 1:14)

What is stirring up within you? Is there a passion or a desire to do something extraordinary? Maybe God is talking with you. Maybe He is stirring you up.

God can talk to us in many ways; one of those is to place passions, desires, and dreams into our hearts. We would do well to consider what we have strong emotions for; maybe it is the stirring that will propel you to something significant.

When He stirs you up, He may well be stirring up others around you. If you find people coming into your life with a similar passion, then get together and pray with them. It could well be that God is stirring the pot.

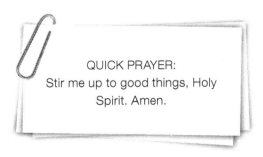

QUICK PRAYER:
Stir me up to good things, Holy
Spirit. Amen.

OCTOBER
20

Pay Fair

"Woe to him who builds his palace by unrighteousness, his upper rooms by injustice, making his own people work for nothing, not paying them for their labor." (JER 22:13)

Workers are worth looking after. You can do nothing by yourself, and those around you who you may employ or lead deserve not only respect and encouragement but also fair pay.

Do you deliberately underpay someone because he or she is young? Do you take advantage of those who fear unemployment or are in financial difficulty? Do you know someone who is worth more in the market but you are profiting from his or her loyalty?

Boss, manager, leader, owner, CEO—God is watching, and He has a heart for the worker.

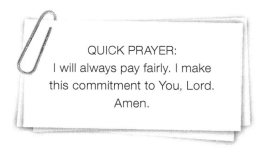

QUICK PRAYER:
I will always pay fairly. I make
this commitment to You, Lord.
Amen.

OCTOBER
21

Pay Well

"'So I will come to put you on trial. I will be quick to testify against sorcerers, adulterers and perjurers, against those who defraud laborers of their wages, who oppress the widows and the fatherless, and deprive the foreigners among you of justice, but do not fear me,' says the Lord Almighty." (Mal 3:5)

If I were to make my list of sins from the most heinous to the least innocuous, sorcerers, adulterers, and perjurers would be pretty high on the list. On the other hand, bosses who don't pay well or avoid their responsibility to pay staff, while obviously not right, would feature lower on the list.

Apparently in this regard among many others, God and I have a different perspective. His view is that these people need to be judged and punished in the same way a sorcerer would. Divination and devil worship are equated with a bad-paying boss.

While business owners and bosses may not defraud laborers and staff, if they endeavor to minimize benefits and pay unreasonably, God is watching and has the worker in mind. With authority comes responsibility.

QUICK PRAYER:
I see You equate not paying fairly with adultery and sorcery; I will give it much more importance than I currently do. Amen.

OCTOBER
22

Negotiate

"Laban said to him, 'Just because you are a relative of mine, should you work for me for nothing? Tell me what your wages should be.'" (GEN 29:15)

There is nothing wrong in negotiating. Don't mistake humility with vulnerability. We are not called to be doormats while we love and serve those around us. If you provide a valuable service or product, ensuring you are well rewarded is an important part of unlocking resources for you and those around you.

Likewise if you are a skilled worker who does a great job serving God with integrity and excellence, ensure you are well rewarded and compensated for your productivity. Linking outcomes to reward is a great way to ensure a share of advantage and blessing. Ask God for insight and favor before you negotiate; He may well surprise you with the outcome.

QUICK PRAYER:
Give me wisdom in my
negotiation and a boldness to
ask. Amen.

God Is Listening

"Look! The wages you failed to pay the workers who mowed your fields are crying out against you. The cries of the harvesters have reached the ears of the Lord Almighty." (Jam 5:4)

God hears the voices of those you have authority over. What would they say about you and how you treat them? God is impartial, and He understands the circumstances, but the question remains.

What do you have in your power to give that you are not giving? There are responsibilities beyond fair pay and conditions. Do you really want to just meet the minimum requirements, or will you go the extra mile for those God has placed at your side?

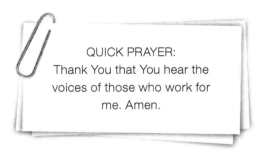

QUICK PRAYER:
Thank You that You hear the voices of those who work for me. Amen.

OCTOBER

24

Be Aware of Circumstances

"Pay them their wages each day before sunset, because they are poor and are counting on it. Otherwise they may cry to the Lord against you, and you will be guilty of sin." (DEU 24:15)

Being aware of people's circumstances is as easy as taking the time to get to know those you work with. Relationship is often cited as unnecessary in the workplace and actively discouraged in many leadership circles.

My view is that if you build relationship, you get to know your people and their strengths and weaknesses. The more you understand them and they understand you, the better you can work together. You can also see areas of development and unlock potential. Plus they will begin to trust you, and you will be able to help them in their circumstances and minister where possible.

QUICK PRAYER:
Help me to be aware of people's circumstances and to act accordingly. Amen.

Equality

"And masters, treat your slaves in the same way. Do not threaten them, since you know that he who is both their Master and yours is in heaven, and there is no favoritism with him." (EPH 6:9)

In a company, there is usually an hierarchy. At the top is the leadership in the C-suite, followed by managers and mid-level leaders down to those who do the real work and then the seemingly more menial roles of packing, serving, or cleaning.

Every link in the chain that is in every company is critical for its success. From the strategy makers to the parcel wrappers, sales to marketing, warehouse to IT, all are important for the company to succeed.

So it is with God. He sees us all equally. CEO and cleaner, manager and sales assistant are all equal in His mind. So how should we treat each other?

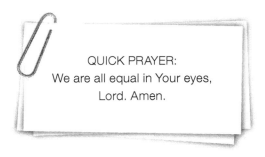

QUICK PRAYER:
We are all equal in Your eyes,
Lord. Amen.

OCTOBER

26

You Are a Blessing

"But Laban said to him, 'If I have found favor in your eyes, please stay. I have learned by divination that the Lord has blessed me because of you.'" (GEN 30:27)

If you are born again, you have become a new creation. These are words we take for granted, but in a very real way, we are now different. Our spirits are now open, and the Holy Spirit indwells us.

In a very real and physical way, we bring the presence of God into our workplace. Regardless of your position at work, God is with you and wants to work through you.

Those around us will receive benefit and blessing just by being associated with us. Is that a source of pride? No, not really. It is probably more of a source of amazement. God will bless your workplace because you are there, if we allow Him to.

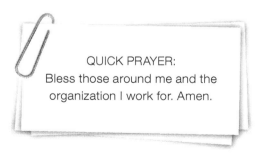

QUICK PRAYER:
Bless those around me and the
organization I work for. Amen.

OCTOBER
27

Blessed by Association

"From the time he put him in charge of his household and of all that he owned, the Lord blessed the household of the Egyptian because of Joseph. The blessing of the Lord was on everything Potiphar had, both in the house and in the field." (GEN 39:5)

When we surrender to God in an area, something extraordinary happens: the kingdom of God is brought to bear in that area. When we surrender to Him at work and offer up to Him all that is in our authority or under our influence, He begins to bless.

We literally bring the blessings of God to all we touch through a surrendered heart and prayerful walk. Those who are around us will experience blessings though association with us.

God is with us, and He also will be with those around us and the company or workplace we minister in. Our work in the world is ministry if it is surrendered and sanctified.

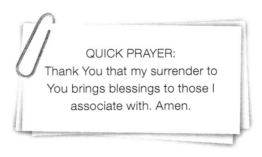

QUICK PRAYER:
Thank You that my surrender to You brings blessings to those I associate with. Amen.

OCTOBER

28

A Faithful Employer

"Each day one ox, six choice sheep and some poultry were prepared for me, and every ten days an abundant supply of wine of all kinds. In spite of all this, I never demanded the food allotted to the governor, because the demands were heavy on these people." (NEH 5:18)

Empathy is rarely held up as an important skill for leaders. To me it is all important that we not only relate as leaders to those around us but also to do so with a high level of empathy.

When we consider others in this light, we begin to get revelation of their concerns and motivators. We can place people in the right roles with the right responsibilities for their skill sets and temperaments.

Equally, when things are not going well or there is need to restructure or discipline, we will be able to do so with a level of understanding and respect that comes from a relationship built on empathy.

QUICK PRAYER:
Help me to treat those You place
under me with respect, dignity,
and empathy. Amen.

Hire Slow

"Like an archer who wounds at random is one who hires a fool or any passer-by." (PRO 26:10)

There is a saying in business that we should hire slow and fire fast. There is actually a lot of truth in what seems like a flippant and perhaps ruthless saying.

Taking the time to ensure that the people we hire are suitable goes way beyond their resume. Yes, we need to hire someone who is able to technically fulfill the positions requirements, but if we value culture, we will go way beyond that.

Great companies are built on certain values and operate in a particular way. If we do not take these soft attributes into account, we will find that the good technical fit may actually be divisive and counterproductive to the whole.

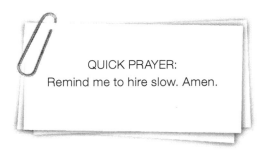

QUICK PRAYER:
Remind me to hire slow. Amen.

OCTOBER

30

Be Faithful

"The workers labored faithfully." (2 Chr 34:12)

If someone were to take a poll on you and ask about your attributes would faithfulness make it to the top? I doubt it would even make my list, yet it is something we should value highly.

Faithfulness is best described as adhering firmly and devotedly to someone or something that elicits or demands one's fidelity. The workers in this Scripture applied themselves to the task at hand with diligence and excellence.

We are called to a way that should compel us to integrity, devotion, excellence, and faithfulness. Fortunately, we serve one who is keen to see us produce such fruit and will ensure we do.

QUICK PRAYER:
There is something wonderful in faithfulness—such an honorable trait. Keep me faithful, Lord.
Amen.

OCTOBER
31

Working with a Brother?

"Those who have believing masters should not show them disrespect just because they are fellow believers. Instead, they should serve them even better because their masters are dear to them as fellow believers and are devoted to the welfare of their slaves." (1 Tim 6:2)

Do you serve someone who is a fellow believer? You know that God sees you as equals and that he or she has a duty of care, but what should our response be when God places another believer in authority over us?

The Scripture is clear that we should go the extra mile to ensure we are model employees and respect and serve them even more than we would normally do. The other person's conduct and walk is not our responsibility; it is between him or her and God. Our responsibility is to serve our leaders as we would Christ, to be a model employee, and to respect their authority.

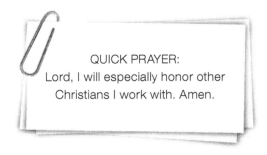

QUICK PRAYER:
Lord, I will especially honor other
Christians I work with. Amen.

NOVEMBER 1

Refreshing

"Like a snow-cooled drink at harvest time is a trustworthy messenger to the one who sends him; he refreshes the spirit of his master." (PRO 25:13)

A cold, crisp, refreshing drink after a hard day's labor is one of life's simple and rewarding pleasures. In this Scripture, that feeling of being refreshed and satisfied is compared to a faithful person who serves us at work.

We all know how great it is to find someone who is motivated and capable who can get on with a job and do excellent work. It is refreshing to see and experience excellence in a task assigned to someone.

Likewise, we should refresh those who have entrusted a task to us. If we operate with excellence and integrity, we will be a blessing to those in authority over us. We are also more likely to be blessed if we are a refreshing blessing.

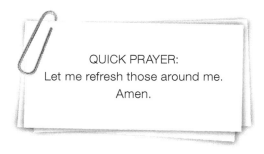

QUICK PRAYER:
Let me refresh those around me.
Amen.

Respect

"All who are under the yoke of slavery should consider their masters worthy of full respect, so that God's name and our teaching may not be slandered." (1 Tim 6:1)

We are called to respect and serve those in authority; I think we are all aware of that responsibility that is inherent in our roles. However, we usually associate the eventual fruit of more authority, promotion, and blessing as the reason why we are asked to act in this way.

While these outcomes often accompany such an approach to work, they are not the primary reason. The key reason is reputation, and not only ours but also God's.

If our witness and words are to be taken seriously, we need to demonstrate a changed life full of reverence and purity and a willingness to serve. These traits are in contrast to the prevailing behaviors of our day. We do not want to bring our witness, words, or God into disrepute.

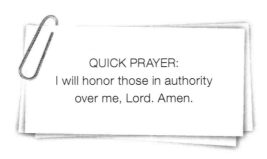

QUICK PRAYER:
I will honor those in authority
over me, Lord. Amen.

NOVEMBER
3

Slander

"Do not slander a servant to their master, or they will curse you, and you will pay for it." (Pro 30:10)

There is something in human nature that finds satisfaction or even delight in gossip, slander, and having a good whine. Today take a listen to the conversations at work and see how often this is the case. If you want a shock, listen to how much you do it yourself.

There is a price we pay when we operate in this way and give into our human natures. It poisons our ability to see clearly regarding the person in question. Our insight and clarity diminish as we cloud out God's thoughts with the words we speak.

We also run a risk that others will repeat what we say and that it will eventually reach the ears of others. If we wish to be deemed trustworthy, we have to avoid slander so that it doesn't come back to get us.

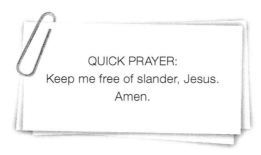

QUICK PRAYER:
Keep me free of slander, Jesus.
Amen.

NOVEMBER
4

Unequally Yoked

"Do not be yoked together with unbelievers. For what do righteousness and wickedness have in common? Or what fellowship can light have with darkness." (2 Cor 6:14)

This Scripture, when taken to the extreme, seems to promote exclusion. We know this is not true because Jesus spent so much time with unbelievers and sinners that He was called one by the righteous folk of the day.

However, there is a point at which we can become entwined contractually or relationally in such a way that the diametrically opposed forces in the heavenlies are joined. Just as oil and water can't mix, so the outcome of being unequally yoked in a partnership can be catastrophic. Make sure you take this truth into account before getting into bed with an unbeliever.

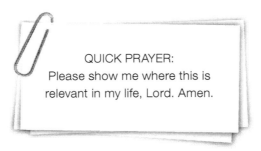

QUICK PRAYER:
Please show me where this is
relevant in my life, Lord. Amen.

NOVEMBER 5

Priority

"Put your outdoor work in order and get your fields ready; after that, build your house." (Pro 24:27)

There is a lot of wisdom in this one very short verse. When we approach a new problem or situation, we have to ascertain the priorities. In this case, the part of the required solution is productive and will ensure the secondary outcome.

If the fields are planted and the income is assured, then time and resources can be allocated to building the house. If the approach is the opposite, the house may well be built but with no food and resources, and disaster would ensue. The outcome could well be the loss of the house.

These two outcomes—failure and success—came from the same set of resources in the same situation with the same people; the only differentiator was the priorities set.

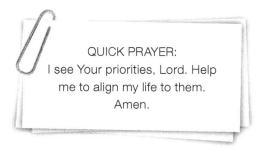

QUICK PRAYER:
I see Your priorities, Lord. Help
me to align my life to them.
Amen.

NOVEMBER 6

Creative Chaos

"Where there are no oxen, the manger is empty, but from the strength of an ox come abundant harvests." (PRO 14:4)

Some people like businesses that operate with mechanistic efficiency and autocratic fervor. Personally, I think they lack soul and personality. More importantly, some cultures will alienate the innovative and entrepreneurial spirit by being overly authoritarian and controlling.

I believe we need to have clear vision and common purpose, but empowerment is an important component of sustainable growth. When we release our people, we unlock their potential. That can have a multiplier effect and create huge momentum.

Does it bring some chaos and mess? Oh yes, definitely, but it also brings success and an empowered workforce.

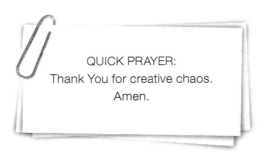

QUICK PRAYER:
Thank You for creative chaos.
Amen.

Serving before Kings

"Do you see someone skilled in their work? They will serve before kings; they will not serve before officials of low rank."
(Pro 22:29)

We are all given a fixed amount of gifts and talents. They are allocated for a purpose, in that we all have a role to play and a part to fulfill. They do come, however, with some responsibility.

Raw talent can only get us so far. The one with some talent will go way past the one with much unless the one with more learns diligence and applies him or herself. We are called to take what God has given us and to hone and develop it with the gifts He has bestowed on us.

Training and learning are not self-interest pastimes; they are the building blocks of servanthood. If we are well equipped and prepared, we can serve effectively and be productive. Then we will be taken to new heights and given even greater opportunity to serve.

QUICK PRAYER:
I commit to developing the skills
You have given me so I may
serve You well. Amen.

What Will Happen Tomorrow?

"Why, you do not even know what will happen tomorrow. What is your life? You are a mist that appears for a little while and then vanishes." (JAM 4:14)

Worry is an insidious emotion. It can get a grip of us and cause us not to sleep and to be concerned for things that may be far into the future. Often they are circumstances that have not occurred and never will.

We have so little control over our lives as it is that self-determination is quite an illusion. When you look from an eternal perspective, we are as the Word says—merely a vapor, here today and gone tomorrow. So what should our reaction be to this truth? Why not enjoy today, this moment, while it lasts and learn to enjoy the journey as much as the destination?

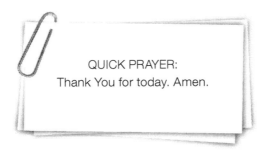

QUICK PRAYER:
Thank You for today. Amen.

NOVEMBER

9

Inheritance

"A good person leaves an inheritance for their children's children, but a sinner's wealth is stored up for the righteous." (PRO 13:22)

We are so interested in the now or the immediate that we rarely think too far ahead. When we look ahead, it may be for a few years ahead or perhaps to plan for retirement.

How many of us look beyond our mortal lives or even beyond the lives of our children? We may not, but God does. He looks to us to have some responsibility to build generational wealth. While many of us will not be able to do that financially, we can all do it spiritually.

As we live our lives and train our children in the way they should go, we pass an inheritance on for generations to come. Take the time to share your walk with your kids and their kids when that time comes. You can bless multiple generations and create a legacy and inheritance of massive value.

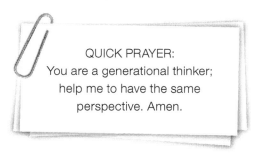

QUICK PRAYER:
You are a generational thinker;
help me to have the same
perspective. Amen.

Inevitability

"In those days Hezekiah became ill and was at the point of death. The prophet Isaiah son of Amoz went to him and said, 'This is what the Lord says: Put your house in order, because you are going to die; you will not recover.'" (Isa 38:1)

There is one thing we will all face regardless of who we are or what we do. It is the great inevitability of it that gives it the absoluteness of perfect certainty; it is going to happen.

Are you prepared to die? First, do you have absolute assurance that you will be welcomed into heaven? Only Jesus can get you there, so make your peace with Him now if you need to get right with God.

Physically have you prepared your family for your passing? Have a will and insurance in place as well as whatever financial and organizational preparation is required. We don't want to think about such things, but we need to prepare for the certainty.

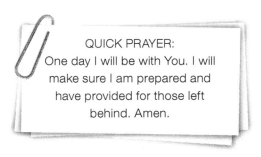

QUICK PRAYER:
One day I will be with You. I will make sure I am prepared and have provided for those left behind. Amen.

NOVEMBER
11

Want to Get Rich?

"Those who want to get rich fall into temptation and a trap and into many foolish and harmful desires that plunge people into ruin and destruction." (1 Tim 6:9)

There is nothing wrong with riches. There is nothing wrong with wealth. Having riches and wealth is a great blessing when they are surrendered and balanced by God.

However, if our motivation in life is to become rich, we can fall into a moral decline to achieve this goal. Many are obsessed to the degree that Godly checks and balances are not countering the greed, and the safely net is not in place.

The result of harmful desires is ruin and destruction—the opposite of the desired outcome. When you have a goal that is not subject to God's control, you will very often pay a hefty price.

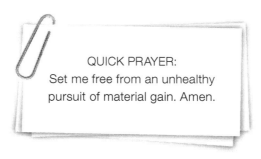

QUICK PRAYER:
Set me free from an unhealthy
pursuit of material gain. Amen.

NOVEMBER 12

Flee

"But you, man of God, flee from all this, and pursue righteousness, godliness, faith, love, endurance and gentleness."
(1 TIM 6:11)

What are the things we should pursue in life? The world and our human nature say we should pursue significance, security, selfish ambition, pleasure, power, wealth, and fortune. That is quite an appealing combination and in essence not all bad.

But what would God have us to pursue? What would He have us chase after and hunt down with all our passion and focus? They are righteousness, godliness, faith, love, gentleness, and everyone's favorite, endurance.

These are the fruit of the Holy Spirit. As we draw close to Him, we begin to reflect and produce this fruit. Consider how we can pursue these God-given goals; it is well worth dwelling on.

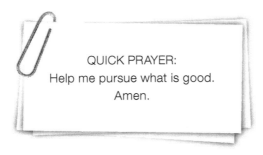

QUICK PRAYER:
Help me pursue what is good.
Amen.

NOVEMBER
13

Saving

"The wise store up choice food and olive oil, but fools gulp theirs down." (PRO 21:20)

Fiscal management has some foundational principles. None is more fundamental that putting aside some of what we earn for a rainy day.

It doesn't get more basic than the wisdom of saving, yet most people in our consumer-driven, materialistic culture spend, spend, spend. Credit cards get maxed, and debt is rife. Just because society behaves in a particular way doesn't mean we have to comply, despite the pressure to do so.

It is the wise who store up and the foolish who gulp their food down. What a strange but apt description of the consumption of what should be put aside. It speaks to me of greed and the carnal nature—something we all need to guard against.

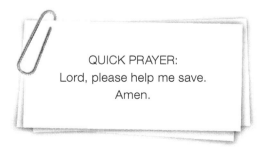

QUICK PRAYER:
Lord, please help me save.
Amen.

Prepare

"They should collect all the food of these good years that are coming and store up the grain under the authority of Pharaoh, to be kept in the cities for food." (GEN 41:35)

The wisdom of God and His revelation to Joseph not only moved a man from prison to prime minister in a day, but it also saved a nation from being destroyed by famine.

This is a dramatic demonstration of the intervention of God through revelation. He talks to those who listen and warns those who will heed His voice. When we take the time to invite Him into our work, we will receive insight and revelation.

While saving a nation is a big deal, God is also interested in the smaller scale. We have every hair on our head numbered and every minute of every day accounted for. Large or small, what we face is of interest to Him.

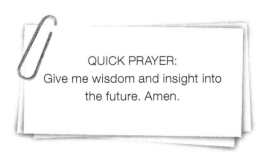

QUICK PRAYER:
Give me wisdom and insight into
the future. Amen.

NOVEMBER
15

Way to Go

"This is what the Lord says—your Redeemer, the Holy One of Israel: 'I am the Lord your God, who teaches you what is best for you, who directs you in the way you should go.'" (Isa 48:17)

Do you ever have a dilemma at work, or in your life? We all do. There are often times when we have choices to make and a number of ways we can go. How often do we consider God's desire for us as we ponder which way to go?

Choosing between a cheese sandwich and a cucumber sandwich may not need an angelic visitation to determine, but a lot of other questions may. Offering a circumstance to God invites clarity and wisdom and His intervention if required.

We have been given a brain and are expected to weigh our options with a certain amount of independence, but many times we would be wise to check with God. Certainly any significant decision should be made in consultation with Him to Whom we have given our lives.

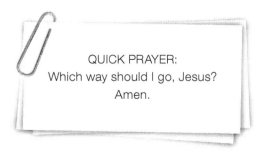

QUICK PRAYER:
Which way should I go, Jesus?
Amen.

NOVEMBER
16

Diversify

"Invest in seven ventures, yes, in eight; you do not know what disaster may come upon the land." (Ecc 11:2)

When we invest, we are advised to make sure we don't put all our eggs in one basket. This is a foundational principle in risk management.

It turns out to be a biblical one as well. There is wisdom in lowering risk because we do not know what the future will hold.

I think this is not only a timely reminder that not all things will go well—and we need to be mindful of that—but also that we are part of a collective. The warning here is that a disaster will come upon the land and by inference potentially affect us. We are not necessarily completely insulated from external influences.

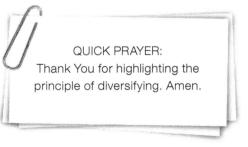

QUICK PRAYER:
Thank You for highlighting the
principle of diversifying. Amen.

NOVEMBER
17

Timing

"There is a time for everything, and a season for every activity under the heavens." (ECC 3:1)

We all have desires in our hearts we would like to see fulfilled. Many of these are God given to help propel us to where we need to be, but there are multiple parts to every call that may be on our lives.

There is a time to sow where we prepare and invest time, money, and effort in getting ourselves ready and equipped. There is a time of winter where absolutely nothing seems to happen. We just have to wait in expectation of spring. Then we move into all He has for us, and we have to put aside what we will need to sow for the next season and reap the reward of our labors.

What we are and more importantly what we do has a specific timeframe. If we leave too early, we will only fail. If we discern the season, we will act appropriately. There is no point in trying to reap in winter or plant in summer.

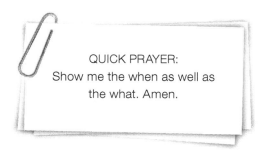

QUICK PRAYER:
Show me the when as well as
the what. Amen.

NOVEMBER 18

Inspection

"Be sure you know the condition of your flocks; give careful attention to your herds." (Pro 27:23)

Whether we are in business, have some authority in the work place, or just have financial oversight over our own income, one thing is very important. In the business of work and life, we can get carried away with all we are doing.

How is your financial state? Do you know what you spend and what your costs are? Do you know what your future requirements may be? Are your investments wisely placed? Are you putting away enough to retire? Are you reducing your debt?

In short, what is coming in, what is going out, and how much do you have? Discipline and robust management of our finances personally or in business can be a painful process to monitor, but monitor it we should.

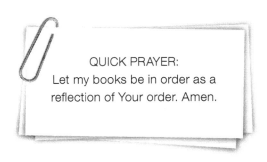

QUICK PRAYER:
Let my books be in order as a reflection of Your order. Amen.

NOVEMBER
19

Order

"But everything should be done in a fitting and orderly way."
(1 COR 14:40)

I quite like a bit of chaos—the thrill of chasing down a deadline and the adrenalin of everyone pulling out all stops to achieve a goal. It is probably not a positive trait, but it is partly how I am wired. If everything is too orderly, I feel uncomfortable.

However, I am not saying chaos is a good thing. We should have an orderly approach because this is a much more effective way of working. All things in order and in their correct place, while a little sterile, is definitely a better way to go.

There is a way that is fitting. This speaks to me of the correct way to do a particular task—one that is the best fit for the objective. In order to achieve that, we need to think about our approach and be a little less reactionary. I think that may be a Godly approach to business.

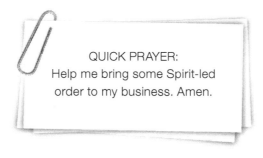

QUICK PRAYER:
Help me bring some Spirit-led
order to my business. Amen.

How Much Is too Much?

"Woe to you who add house to house and join field to field till no space is left and you live alone in the land." (Isa 5:8)

Is there anything wrong with building a house? No, nor is there anything wrong with building many. The same is true of land and the acquisition of real estate. So why is there woe attached to this case?

There are two outcomes here: there is no space left, and the person building is left all alone. What is the lesson here? I think there are two. Our personal lives can be impacted when we build and work to acquire at the expense of all else. When we have no balance, not only to be consume resources and there is nothing left for other use, and we also can burn off all the good will we need to maintain relationship. We end up with a lot of stuff but with no one to share it with.

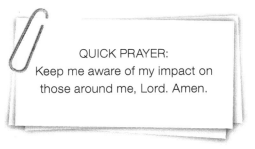

QUICK PRAYER:
Keep me aware of my impact on
those around me, Lord. Amen.

No Good!

"'It's no good, it's no good!' says the buyer—then goes off and boasts about the purchase." (PRO 20:14)

This is such a true proverb. Whenever I have been involved in negotiations in business, I have often seen this behavior. God understands the motives and behaviors of men.

It is good to know that God has our best in mind. When you are involved in any kind of negotiation or deal, why not ask for His wisdom and insight? You may be surprised by the outcome.

God is interested in the outcome because it impacts us, His children. When we ask for His involvement, He is always there to be a part of what we are doing. God is often left out because we think He is not interested in some part of our lives. He is enormously interested in every aspect of our work life—even deals.

QUICK PRAYER:
Give me Your wisdom in the deal please, Lord. Amen.

Women in Business

"She considers a field and buys it; out of her earnings she plants a vineyard." (Pro 31:16)

Jesus was, and is, one of the greatest liberators of women in history—so much so that early writings see the 'Christian Way' as a political movement rather than a religious one. A key reason for this was the empowerment of women. In the society of the time, women were regarded as little more than chattels.

The clearest example we have of a great businessperson in the Bible is the Proverbs 31 woman. Here is a wonderful example of wisdom, application, diligence, and fiscal responsibility.

God is definitely into having women in business, so let's not get in His way with some of our religiosity. There is no glass ceiling in God's economy; He will exalt women into leadership roles if they allow Him to do so.

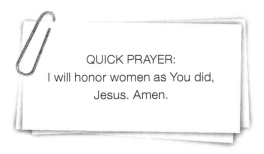

QUICK PRAYER:
I will honor women as You did,
Jesus. Amen.

NOVEMBER
23

No Interest

"If you lend money to one of my people among you who is needy, do not treat it like a business deal; charge no interest."
(Exo 22:25)

When we have a position of authority and substance, it comes with a level of responsibility. When we are entering into a deal or project with one another, we have a duty of care to consider their circumstances.

This is no truer than when we are involved in the family of faith. That is not to say we should always do everything for believers at a discount or for free, but we should consider the impact on the other party and his or her ability to pay.

Sometimes it is not meant to be a purely commercial business deal; God may have something else in mind. He may be calling you to bless someone in the midst of your business dealings.

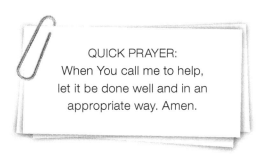

QUICK PRAYER:
When You call me to help,
let it be done well and in an
appropriate way. Amen.

Crazy Love

"But love your enemies, do good to them, and lend to them without expecting to get anything back. Then your reward will be great, and you will be children of the Most High, because he is kind to the ungrateful and wicked." (Luk 6:35)

I do struggle with God's logic sometimes. Here again we are called to walk in a way that on the surface is just plain crazy. Why would you do good to your enemies? Lending to someone who hates you just lacks plain common sense.

Yet it is God who says this is the best and wisest way, so who are we to argue with our Creator? He works on the heart of man in strange and mysterious ways. When we walk in forgiveness and mercy, we see God's hand at work in our own lives. When we do things His way, we are freed from the dark places in our own souls.

God treats the Godly and ungodly with kindness, and so should we.

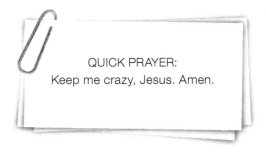

QUICK PRAYER:
Keep me crazy, Jesus. Amen.

NOVEMBER
25

Not Even a Hint

"But among you there must not be even a hint of sexual immorality, or of any kind of impurity, or of greed, because these are improper for God's holy people." (EPH 5:3)

We are all sexual beings, and at work we spend a lot of time with others. There is always temptation and relationship risk when we work closely with others.

Where should we place the boundaries to protect ourselves and our partners? God places the line way back beyond where we might think. There should not even be a hint of immorality—not even the slightest innuendo or flirt.

When you take care of the way it looks, you actually take care of the way it is. If it can be interpreted wrongly, then give it a wide berth. Too many have succumbed to a workplace affair. If you are in danger of being snared, then flee before it is too late.

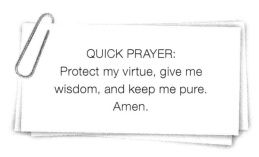

QUICK PRAYER:
Protect my virtue, give me
wisdom, and keep me pure.
Amen.

NOVEMBER
26

A Price to Pay

"A number who had practiced sorcery brought their scrolls together and burned them publicly. When they calculated the value of the scrolls, the total came to fifty thousand drachmas." (Act 19:19)

When we recognize that God is calling us in a certain direction, or asking us to make some adjustment in our lives, there can be consequences that cost us in some way or another.

The cost could be in relationships with those who don't want to give up some types of behavior. It could be in time or resources that are given to other areas. He may be calling us to give up some form of income or lifestyle that will cost us financially.

Giving up behaviors or items that do not honor God and are the result of true repentance demonstrate a real encounter and a changed life. What is God asking you to do today?

QUICK PRAYER:
I realize repentance or a change can cost me. Give me the strength to change. Amen.

NOVEMBER
27

Restitution

"The one who struck the blow will not be held liable if the other can get up and walk around outside with a staff; however, the guilty party must pay the injured person for any loss of time and see that the victim is completely healed." (Exo 21:19)

God is a God of forgiveness, and when He forgives, we are forgiven completely. However, the consequences for our sin often still remain. Despite being forgiven, we may have outcomes that need to be addressed.

While we are not under the Law and do not need to make amends through a legalistic framework, we still have a duty to show acts in keeping with repentance. These are not to gain forgiveness but are evidence of it being received.

We can't ask God for forgiveness and then ignore the impact of our sin. We have a duty to take care of addressing the consequences in gratefulness for the forgiveness we have freely received.

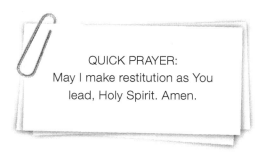

QUICK PRAYER:
May I make restitution as You
lead, Holy Spirit. Amen.

Den of Robbers

"Jesus entered the temple courts and drove out all who were buying and selling there. He overturned the tables of the money changers and the benches of those selling doves. 'It is written,' he said to them, "My house will be called a house of prayer," but you are making it "a den of robbers.""
(MAT 21:12–13)

Gentle Jesus, meek and mild. We have a tainted view of Jesus handed down and watered down by generations of religion. It is reflected in the imagery we use of a pale, clean, somewhat feminine portrayal of Jesus.

He was a Jewish carpenter, rugged and masculine. He also got angry yet did not sin. In this Scripture, He threw many people out of the temple, and I am sure they didn't want to go and did not go quietly.

There is a place for anger and strong action—in particular here when He was jealous and zealous for His House.

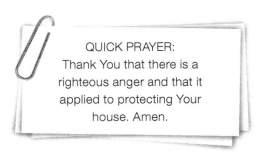

QUICK PRAYER:
Thank You that there is a righteous anger and that it applied to protecting Your house. Amen.

NOVEMBER
29

Can't Get No Satisfaction

"Whoever loves money never has enough; whoever loves wealth is never satisfied with their income. This too is meaningless."
(Ecc 5:10)

If only I can have this or that, then I will be satisfied. Have you noticed that the latest and greatest tool or toy from a few years back now no longer has the same appeal?

Consumerism is built on waves of dissatisfaction. We always need to replace the last favorite thing with the next new latest and greatest toy. The same is true for wealth and money in general.

Check out some really wealthy people. Do they look happy to you? If wealth truly made people happy, the more they have, the happier they would be. This is patently not true, so let's keep our eyes focused on what truly satisfies.

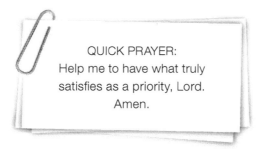

QUICK PRAYER:
Help me to have what truly
satisfies as a priority, Lord.
Amen.

Settle and Move On

"Settle matters quickly with your adversary who is taking you to court. Do it while you are still together on the way, or your adversary may hand you over to the judge, and the judge may hand you over to the officer, and you may be thrown into prison." (MAT 5:25)

If you are in business or in any level of authority in the workplace, there will be disagreements and even legal threats. How are we to face these things, and what should our response be?

We are advised to settle quickly to make sure we don't expose ourselves to greater consequences. There are two options; we are either right or wrong. However, regardless of our view of the situation, we should not place ourselves at risk in court unnecessarily.

Pride can be a great motivator, and it will drive us to push to the limits whether we are right or wrong. The consequences of letting this dangerous emotion get the better of us are self-evident.

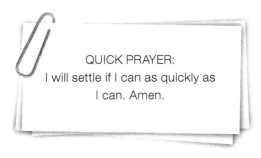

QUICK PRAYER:
I will settle if I can as quickly as
I can. Amen.

DECEMBER
1

Christian Counsel

"If any of you has a dispute with another, do you dare to take it before the ungodly for judgment instead of before the Lord's people?" (1 Cor 6:1)

Christians are always having splits and spats with each other. It is probably not a good witness, and God is not particularly impressed with this kind of behavior. He is into unity and even commands a blessing when we dwell together in one accord.

When we have divisions and disagreements between believers, how should they be resolved? If we are in a family of faith, perhaps we should look to our own internal resources before going to court. God has placed people of wisdom in our midst who are able to help resolve issues between brothers. At least give it a chance before parading our failures before unbelievers.

QUICK PRAYER:
Forgive me for resorting to ungodly wisdom to settle a case.
Amen.

Storytellers

"In their greed these teachers will exploit you with fabricated stories. Their condemnation has long been hanging over them, and their destruction has not been sleeping." (2 Pet 2:3)

Sometimes things are not as they seem. People's motives may not be clear as we relate to them in a workplace setting. Those slick storytellers come in all shapes and sizes, and we should be wary of their persuasive talk.

There are many who would look to exploit you for any number of reasons. Fortunately, we serve someone who sees the very heart of every person. He can expose the thoughts of man, and we should be careful to listen to Him.

If you don't feel a peace about something, whether it be a person, decision, or situation, take the time to clarify. God can use those inner feelings to show you something beyond the smooth sales pitch.

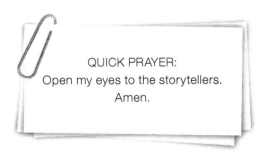

QUICK PRAYER:
Open my eyes to the storytellers.
Amen.

DECEMBER
3

Idols

"But their idols are silver and gold, made by human hands."
(Psa 115:4)

Idols come in all sorts of shapes, sizes, and guises. An idol is simply something we worship before God. You probably don't have a statue in your house that you burn incense and sacrifice to every morning, yet that doesn't mean you don't have idols.

An idol can be work, career, a relationship, money, cars, or leisure; many, many things can be idols. When you have the choice to do it God's way and something else prevails, the chances are an idol is not far away.

Even our religious form worship or serving God can be an idol if it comes between us and God. The Bible warns of a time where there is a form of godliness but one that denies God's power.

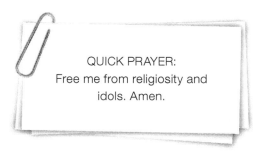

QUICK PRAYER:
Free me from religiosity and
idols. Amen.

Favoritism

"Who shows no partiality to princes and does not favor the rich over the poor, for they are all the work of his hands?" (JOB 34:19)

We are the product of the society we live in. We cannot escape the worldview and attitudes we are raised with. Society's norms are almost absorbed by osmosis. Many of the places we live are quite egalitarian, others are structured into classes and sects.

As believers we are called to one standard regardless of where we live, who we are, or what our society accepts as normal. We are to show no partiality or favor to those in high social positions over those who are deemed to be of lesser status.

We are all equal in the eyes of God, rich or poor, because we were all created by His hand.

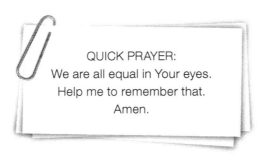

QUICK PRAYER:
We are all equal in Your eyes.
Help me to remember that.
Amen.

DECEMBER
5

Pity and Favoritism

"And do not show favoritism to a poor person in a lawsuit."
(Exo 23:3)

We are to look after the poor and to heed the call for justice. However, if we find ourselves in a position where we have to judge between a rich person and a poor person in a dispute, we are given a clear instruction.

While Robin Hood may have been deemed a hero for robbing from the rich and giving to the poor, he was still a thief. If we are to judge without partiality and to treat people equally, then this applies to rich and poor alike.

While we are to pity the poor and help where we can, this doesn't mean being unreasonable to the rich. We are not to favor the poor over the rich but to treat them with equal respect and regard.

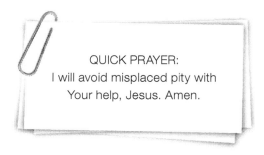

QUICK PRAYER:
I will avoid misplaced pity with
Your help, Jesus. Amen.

DECEMBER
6

Why Tax?

"This is also why you pay taxes, for the authorities are God's servants, who give their full time to governing." (ROM 13:6)

Taxes are not one of my favorite things. I am sure not many look forward to tax time and to paying their dues. The temptation to cut corners and engage in evasive behavior can be strong.

God says we are to pay taxes when taxes are due, and this Scripture gives us a reason. He has appointed those over us to govern and be in authority. While we may question His wisdom in whom He has appointed, the message is clear.

God has appointed authorities, and we are to honor them and their authority by paying our taxes.

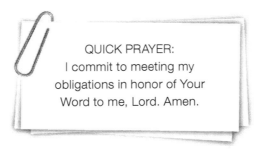

QUICK PRAYER:
I commit to meeting my
obligations in honor of Your
Word to me, Lord. Amen.

DECEMBER
7

Take Action

"This is what the Lord says to you, house of David: "'Administer justice every morning; rescue from the hand of the oppressor the one who has been robbed, or my wrath will break out and burn like fire because of the evil you have done—burn with no one to quench it.'"" (JER 21:12)

There are times when we are touched by stories of injustice. When at work, we can hear of people who are not getting a fair hearing or where justice is not being applied. While being moved is good, it is action that is required.

This Scripture is very strong. God sees and wants justice to prevail. It is never easy to speak up and make a stand. You may pay a price, but God will be pleased as you stand up for what is right, just, and true.

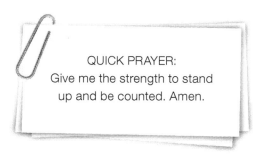

QUICK PRAYER:
Give me the strength to stand
up and be counted. Amen.

DECEMBER
8

Ruin

"The wealth of the rich is their fortified city, but poverty is the ruin of the poor." (Pro 10:15)

There are good things that come with wealth. While there are warnings about wealth, they are usually associated with our attitude toward it and the price we pay to gain it.

When our heart is right before God and we have wealth in balance, it is a blessing from God. It cannot only provide but also protect. It is like a fortified city in that it can bless and protect many. It can be a source of economic prosperity to many people and a safe haven for those who need it.

Poverty can be ruinous and lead to many ills. How we manage our finances and our attitude to money and provision are important to us, and they are important to God. He understands the impact of plenty and of lack.

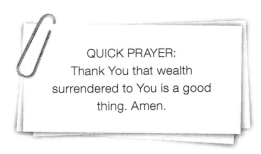

QUICK PRAYER:
Thank You that wealth
surrendered to You is a good
thing. Amen.

DECEMBER
9

Obey and Serve

"If they obey and serve him, they will spend the rest of their days in prosperity and their years in contentment." (Job 36:11)

We all would like some prosperity and contentment. Being followers of Jesus doesn't make us any less capable of enjoying the good things of life. These are good and worthwhile things. They are gifts from the One we serve. God says that He wants to give us this kind of life.

What do we have to do to receive these desirable gifts? We have to be obedient and we have to serve. If we seek first the Kingdom of God, which is wherever He is King and His will is done, then these other things will be added to us.

When we serve, we put His priorities ahead of our own and treat others with respect and deference. As we obey Him and serve His will, we will gain our heart's desires.

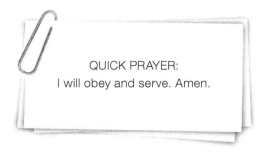

QUICK PRAYER:
I will obey and serve. Amen.

DECEMBER
10

Perspective

"For they will take nothing with them when they die, their splendor will not descend with them." (PSA 49:17)

Naked we came into the world, and empty handed we will depart from it. We can take nothing with us except the souls we will meet again that we had some eternal impact on.

All the houses, nice clothes, cars, gadgets, and toys will all be gone when we face our Maker in eternity. There are no status symbols, no trappings of wealth, no authority, and no power— just us alone before Him.

Our salvation is assured as we plead the blood of Him who died for us and paid the penalty we would otherwise have to endure. It is a perspective worth dwelling on when we assess what is really important in this all-too-brief life.

QUICK PRAYER:
One day I will be face to face with You. Thank You for the wonderful gift of Your salvation.
Amen.

DECEMBER

11

Exchange

"What good will it be for someone to gain the whole world, yet forfeit their soul? Or what can anyone give in exchange for their soul?" (Mat 16:26)

When we have an eternal perspective, our worldly trappings come into their true perspective. How important is our salvation and the salvation of others.

The Bible suggests that not even if we gained all the wealth in the world would it be worth losing our souls. Do we really take this perspective, or do we give too much weight to wealth and power?

Those we talk to about Jesus, or should be talking to about Jesus, are poor, blind, and naked without Him and will go to a Christless eternity if they don't hear, repent, and get saved. It doesn't matter how wealthy they are; it is of no value.

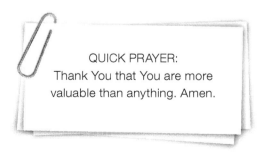

QUICK PRAYER:
Thank You that You are more
valuable than anything. Amen.

Friends

"The poor are shunned even by their neighbors, but the rich have many friends." (Pro 14:20)

Friends are a good thing. I am a social being, and I enjoy others' company and meeting with friends. But are we selective in our friendships? Do we exclude the less fortunate or those who have some social stigma?

Alternatively, do we pursue friendships with people who are of influence or standing so we can gain some respect? We may even do so without realizing our true motivations.

Jesus was called a sinner because He associated with the wrong kind of people. He is our example, and we would do well to emulate Him even if we receive the same tarnished reputation.

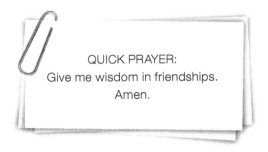

QUICK PRAYER:
Give me wisdom in friendships.
Amen.

DECEMBER
13

Certainty

"Cast but a glance at riches, and they are gone, for they will surely sprout wings and fly off to the sky like an eagle." (Pro 23:5)

We chase after investments and money to enjoy a lifestyle and security. While these are not necessarily bad things, they are a false hope if they are our only source of security.

Wealth can disappear in an instant. Share markets crash, asset bubbles burst, and investments go sour. Economies change; banks and companies fail; and war, revolution, or famine can destroy entire counties.

True peace and contentment coupled with assurance and security can only be found in the One Who never changes and Who is the Rock of Ages.

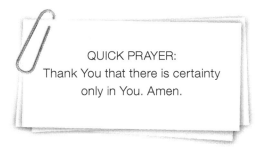

QUICK PRAYER:
Thank You that there is certainty
only in You. Amen.

Redemption

"For you know that it was not with perishable things such as silver or gold that you were redeemed from the empty way of life handed down to you from your ancestors." (1 Pet 1:18)

We were bought with an incredible price. The blood of Jesus is the most precious commodity in all time and in all eternity. With the spilling of that blood, we were redeemed from eternal banishment, and that sacrifice ushered us into the presence of God, free from sin and death.

How much does God value you if He would not spare His only Son to secure your salvation? You were so precious to Him that He redeemed you to Himself not with mere gold or silver but with the most precious substance in the universe.

It was a massive price to pay, but it reflects the love God has for you.

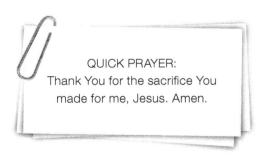

QUICK PRAYER:
Thank You for the sacrifice You
made for me, Jesus. Amen.

DECEMBER

15

Profit and Loss

"But whatever were gains to me I now consider loss for the sake of Christ. What is more, I consider everything a loss because of the surpassing worth of knowing Christ Jesus my Lord, for whose sake I have lost all things. I consider them garbage, that I may gain Christ." (PHI 3:7–8)

Value is a concept that is important in all businesses. We need to express true value to our clients and customers to ensure their business and to get them to purchase our products or services.

How we value something determines what we will pay for it. When we value something very highly, we will sacrifice a lot to attain it. Here Paul puts his previous life and wealth into perspective compared to the value of knowing Jesus. He counted all his previous gains and what he had lost as pure rubbish—just nothing—compared with the relationship he now had with Jesus. Are we that committed?

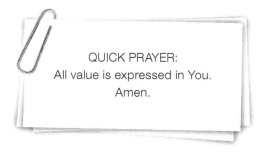

QUICK PRAYER:
All value is expressed in You.
Amen.

One Hundredfold

"Isaac planted crops in that land and the same year reaped a hundredfold, because the Lord blessed him." (GEN 26:12)

How do you know that the Lord has blessed you? How about receiving a hundredfold return on your capital or labor? I think that would be a good sign that God's hand is on us at work. That is a one million–dollar return on a ten thousand–dollar investment.

If God is the same yesterday, today, and tomorrow, He is more than able to bless you in this way. Is it presumptuous to ask Him to bless us in this way? Do we believe He is willing and able to bless us?

God wants to bless us as we move in faith and expectation to receive what He has planned for us. When we do this, our lives will bear the mark of God's blessing.

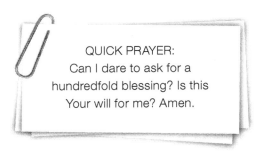

QUICK PRAYER:
Can I dare to ask for a hundredfold blessing? Is this Your will for me? Amen.

Honor

"Then Pharaoh took his signet ring from his finger and put it on Joseph's finger. He dressed him in robes of fine linen and put a gold chain around his neck." (GEN 41:42)

Who was it that put Joseph in charge of Egypt? Could a prisoner in jail really orchestrate his release, let alone his promotion to prime minister of all Egypt? Of course not; we all know it is only God who can move this way and promote a man to this kind of position and influence.

Just as God gave honor to Joseph, He can and will give honor to us as we serve Him in the marketplace. When we choose to go God's way and be obedient and faithful to Him, we may pay a price.

Ultimately, though, God's true purpose will show through because He honors His servants and those who are obedient to His calling. I am sure Joseph would have preferred to miss out on the jail experience, but it all worked together for good.

QUICK PRAYER:
Thank You for the level of honor
and influence You have already
placed on me. Amen.

Blessing

- -

"He died at a good old age, having enjoyed long life, wealth and honor. His son Solomon succeeded him as king."
(1 Chr 29:28)

Here is a great example of what it means to be blessed. We don't have to be super-spiritual about this. God understands we live in a physical world and have desires that have physical manifestations that are required to fulfill them.

Would long life, wealth, and honor be a reasonable definition of a successful life and the blessing of God? Perhaps we could add fulfilling relationships and good health to the list.

Whatever we would consider a blessing that would be a desire of our heart and honoring to the God we serve is a request we can lay before the throne. Ask for a blessing today, not out of a sense that you are worthy, because none of us are, but out of a relationship with a heavenly Father Who would like to bless us.

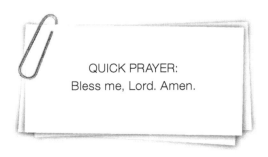

QUICK PRAYER:
Bless me, Lord. Amen.

DECEMBER
19

Delight

"May those who delight in my vindication shout for joy and gladness; may they always say, 'The Lord be exalted, who delights in the well-being of his servant.'" (Psa 35:27)

We have all come from different backgrounds and experiences of what a father is like. Some fathers were loving and kind, others brutal or even absent, but all were fallible and human. What about our concept of our heavenly Father? It has to be impacted by the example of our earthly father.

Our concept of God is also molded by tradition or maybe by religion or myth. Most of us underestimate the love God has for us. Many see Him as a capricious deity Who is ready to punish.

God delights in me and you. Delight is such an all-encompassing and emotive word that we cannot mistake it for just a passing interest. He delights in our wellbeing. He wants and loves to see us doing very well indeed.

QUICK PRAYER:
Thank You that You delight in me
and in my wellbeing. Amen.

DECEMBER
20

Riches for God?

"In a loud voice they were saying: 'Worthy is the Lamb, who was slain, to receive power and wealth and wisdom and strength and honor and glory and praise!'" (REV 5:12)

When they worship Jesus in heaven, they attribute many things to Him. Praise, glory, and honor are due to Him, and He is worthy to receive this adoration. They also praise Him, saying He should receive strength and wisdom, which all come from Him.

They start with saying that Jesus is worthy to receive power and wealth. God has all wealth and all power, all honor, all strength, and all wisdom. If we are subject to the kingdom of God, we worship by acknowledging these are all His and that He is worthy.

Laying down our wealth, authority, and power to Him is part of our worship and acknowledging that He is worthy.

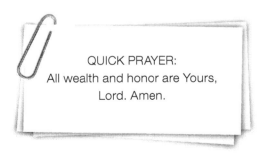

QUICK PRAYER:
All wealth and honor are Yours,
Lord. Amen.

DECEMBER
21

Deceitfulness

"The seed falling among the thorns refers to someone who hears the word, but the worries of this life and the deceitfulness of wealth choke the word, making it unfruitful." (Mat 13:22)

Our enemy uses many ways to distract us from the word of truth planted in us by the Holy Spirit. This example is one Jesus used when talking about the sower and how the Word of God is received in many hearts.

Thorns and weeds of worldliness can grow up and choke the Word of God and the beginnings of what He is doing in our lives. Wealth unfettered with the constraints of a generous heart and application of the Word of God can be a dangerous deception.

Materialism and the pursuit of wealth and advancement can literally choke the life out of God's plan and out of your spiritual life. Possessions and wealth are not wrong in themselves, but when not tempered in surrender to God, they work against you.

QUICK PRAYER:
Please protect me from
worldliness. Amen.

DECEMBER
22

Camel Eye

"Again I tell you, it is easier for a camel to go through the eye of a needle than for someone who is rich to enter the kingdom of God." (MAT 19:24)

This is a somewhat distressing concept and shows just how blinding wealth and riches can be. People who have all they need are less likely to acknowledge the call of their hearts to the Savior. They are also able to be busy in a thousand distractions and find pleasure in many other pastimes.

But we can rest assured that nothing is impossible for God, and He is completely able and willing to touch the heart of the wealthy just as He can touch the heart of the poor and needy. Both are equally lost, and both are equally in need of a Savior.

When we think of evangelism, we must not discount the powerful, rich, and wealthy. They need Jesus, and He loves them just as much as anyone else. Nobody is beyond His reach.

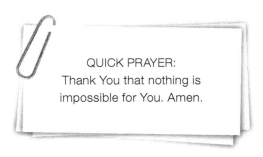

QUICK PRAYER:
Thank You that nothing is
impossible for You. Amen.

DECEMBER

23

The Birds Are Listening

"Do not revile the king even in your thoughts, or curse the rich in your bedroom, because a bird in the sky may carry your words, and a bird on the wing may report what you say." (ECC 10:20)

I don't think the birds are really listening to what we are saying, but the impetus of this word is that we should act as though they were.

We are all placed at work with someone in authority over us. Our leaders are not always as we may want them to be; in fact, some may be downright awful. While we do not condone any unreasonable behavior, we are called to respect those God places in authority over us.

Part of that responsibility is not to revile or curse them. If we do talk to others unkindly or unreasonably behind the backs of our superiors, this Scripture suggests they may find out.

Even if they don't, the words we speak denigrate our own relationships with others as they see how we treat other people behind their backs. We also poison our own hearts and reinforce our character judgments, which may or may not be correct.

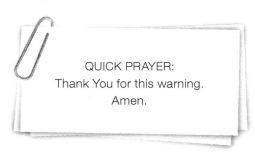

QUICK PRAYER:
Thank You for this warning.
Amen.

Pretense

* *

"One person pretends to be rich, yet has nothing; another pretends to be poor, yet has great wealth." (Pro 13:7)

People are not necessarily who they seem to be. We assume so much by what people are wearing or what they are driving. Those at work who seem to have everything may be on the verge of bankruptcy. Some who look like they have nothing at all my be wealthy beyond all measure.

We need to look to the heart and disregard the outward appearance. We should judge people by their fruit, not their appearance. Someone my need to create a persona to be comfortable and keep his or her true self inside, deeply locked away.

When we know Jesus, we have to put away the entire pretense and be who we really are. It is okay to be vulnerable and be who God has made us to be. As we drop all pretense, we truly become all God has designed us to be.

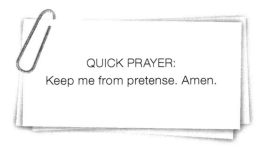

QUICK PRAYER:
Keep me from pretense. Amen.

DECEMBER
25

Hidden Treasure

"The kingdom of heaven is like treasure hidden in a field. When a man found it, he hid it again, and then in his joy went and sold all he had and bought that field." (MAT 13:44)

What would you give everything you own for? What value would you prescribe to an object that you would sell absolutely everything you own just to get a hold of?

Jesus talked about the treasure hidden in the field as being like the kingdom of God. It was an analogy described to encourage us to see the real importance associated with the gospel.

Jesus and the message He gave us of salvation and the coming of the kingdom of God are to be valued beyond all we own. Everything we have and all that we are is to be committed to the cause of Christ. The value we prescribe to Him can never be enough; He is beyond the value of creation itself.

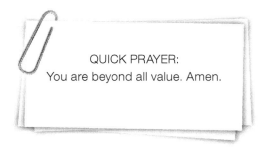

QUICK PRAYER:
You are beyond all value. Amen.

Double Portion Please

"Instead of your shame you will receive a double portion, and instead of disgrace you will rejoice in your inheritance. And so you will inherit a double portion in your land, and everlasting joy will be yours." (Isa 61:7)

I love this word; it is such an encouragement to me. Here is a wonderful and endearing picture of the heart of God to restore. He will take our shame and replace it with a blessing double the size of what was lost.

He will take the disgrace we may have experienced, and it will be replaced with rejoicing in the abundance of His blessing and provision. If you have experienced failure at work, there is hope in these words.

Not only will we receive twice as much as we would have originally had things gone well, but the joy will be everlasting. It will be a blessing not only for this world but for the one beyond out into eternity for ever and ever—blessing, abundance, and joy.

QUICK PRAYER:
Thank You that failure does
not preclude a great blessing.
Amen.

DECEMBER

27

Marked

"It also forced all people, great and small, rich and poor, free and slave, to receive a mark on their right hands or on their foreheads." (Rev 13:16)

The idea of a mark without which no man can buy or sell is one we are asked to look out for as a sign of the coming end and the rise of the antichrist. The Word says we are to have wisdom to understand the significance and the season when this occurs.

While there is nothing wrong with this kind of technology, its application in this case will be a test for all believers. We are told clearly not to take the mark, and that will divide those who are obedient and those who are not.

It will be a time of trouble, difficulty, and persecution but one we can rejoice in and endure because we will then know that the end is near and our Lord and Savior will soon return. Meanwhile, embrace the technology, but when the time comes, reject the mark.

QUICK PRAYER:
You said this requires wisdom.
Give me what I need to
understand. Amen.

DECEMBER
28

Transformers

"And we, who with unveiled faces all reflect the Lord's glory, are being transformed into his likeness with ever-increasing glory, which comes from the Lord, who is the Spirit." (2 COR 3:18)

If work is from God, why is it so hard sometimes? When God begins to transform us, He doesn't sprinkle dust from heaven; He applies pressure and heat. Like a diamond needs pressure to be created and just as gold is refined in fire, so too do we need adversity to grow godly character.

We have two options when the heat gets turned up: resist and achieve nothing or surrender to God, press into Him, and choose to react in His ways. The dross rises quickly to the surface, and we need to let Jesus heal us and transform us into His own image.

This is not a pleasant process, yet it will transform us to be available for His purposes and plan. We need to cooperate with His plan and not resist the change process. Who are we as clay to tell the Potter He is not making us correctly?

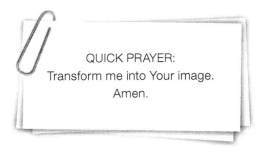

QUICK PRAYER:
Transform me into Your image.
Amen.

Powerful

"But you shall receive power (ability, efficiency, and might) when the Holy Spirit has come upon you, and you shall be My witnesses in Jerusalem and all Judea and Samaria and to the ends (the very bounds) of the earth." (ACT 1:8 AMP)

When we are at work, we sometimes assume that we can do it all ourselves—that somehow this is not God's domain but ours. In our busy schedules, we find little time to contemplate on either God's will or His agenda for our work day.

We trust in our own abilities, experience, and knowledge, and they probably serve us quite well most of the time. But there is another way where we will be anointed, appointed, and empowered by God.

When we ask the Holy Spirit to empower us, we receive power, ability, efficiency, and might. These four gifts are to achieve our purpose, and we will be witnesses for Him not only in our own city but also throughout the world.

QUICK PRAYER:
Fill me afresh, Holy Spirit, and empower me to do Your work.
Amen.

Free

"Come, all you who are thirsty, come to the waters; and you who have no money, come, buy and eat! Come, buy wine and milk without money and without cost." (ISA 55:1)

What a wonderful picture of a God who will provide for all our needs and satisfy the desires of our hearts. Freely given in abundance are water for the thirsty and sustenance without us giving anything.

This unilateral giving from a loving God is a demonstration of the heart of God, Who is not looking for anything in return. He wants to provide not only water that will ensure we live and milk to help us grow but also wine for us to enjoy.

It is an invitation to the thirsty—to those of us who recognize our need and that it is only in God that we can find true rest for our souls and satisfaction that knows no bounds or ends.

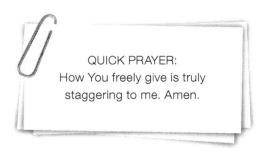

QUICK PRAYER:
How You freely give is truly
staggering to me. Amen.

DECEMBER

31

God's Way of Working

"Servants, respectfully obey your earthly masters but always with an eye to obeying the real master, Christ. Don't just do what you have to do to get by, but work heartily, as Christ's servants doing what God wants you to do. And work with a smile on your face, always keeping in mind that no matter who happens to be giving the orders, you're really serving God. Good work will get you good pay from the Master, regardless of whether you are slave or free. Masters, it's the same with you. No abuse, please, and no threats. You and your servants are both under the same Master in heaven. He makes no distinction between you and them. And that about wraps it up. God is strong, and He wants you strong. So take everything the Master has set out for you, well-made weapons of the best materials. And put them to use so you will be able to stand up to everything the Devil throws your way. This is no afternoon athletic contest that we'll walk away from and forget about in a couple of hours. This is for keeps, a life-or-death fight to the finish against the Devil and all his angels." (Eph 6:5–12 MSG)

QUICK PRAYER:
I commit myself and my work into Your hands, Lord. Bless me and guide me according to Your Word. Amen.

ABOUT THE AUTHOR

Mark Bilton BSc, DipBus, MBA

Mark has extensive experience working as a CEO, director, and managing director in private, multinational, and publicly listed companies. His specialty is creating value through strategy, vision, and culture, and he describes himself as a "change catalyst." His most recent position was as the CEO of Hagemeyer Brands Australia, which was transformed and divested on behalf of listed multinational French owners Rexel in less than two years.

Mark was recently appointed to the Gloria Jean's Coffees board, helping to oversee 1,000 coffee houses in over 30 countries. Mark has held numerous commercial and not-for-profit directorships on industry, charitable trust, leadership, international missions, and educational bodies.

Mark recently was presented the Terry Plochman Award for being the world's best YPO Forum Officer in front of over 2,000 CEOs in Denver by the premier leadership body the Young Presidents Organization.

He has a passion for business and for Christians in the marketplace. His online ministry, Called to Business (www.CalledtoBusiness.com), uses social media to "encourage and equip Christian business leaders to be effective in the marketplace." Mark has a master's in business administration, a post-graduate diploma in business, and a bachelor's of science.

He has been married to Helen for 20 years, has three young children, and lives in Sydney.

RECOMMENDED RESOURCES

Called to Business: www.CalledtoBusiness.com

Monday Matters, author Mark Bilton's online ministry to "encourage and equip Christians to be effective in the workplace." You will find many resources in this ministry, including a powerful weekly biblical business e-message that you can receive in your e-mail.

You can find *Called to Business* on the social media sites listed below:

- www.Facebook.com/CalledtoBusiness
- www.Twitter.com/Calledto
- www.YouTube.com/CalledtoBusiness

Monday Matters: www.MondayMatters.net

This is the home of the *Monday Matters* books and resources. You can find *Monday Matters* on the following social media sites:

- www.Facebook.com/MondayMatters
- www.Twitter.com/MondayMatters

Mark Bilton: www.MarkBilton.com

Monday Matters author Mark Bilton's personal blog.

You can find Mark Bilton on the social media sites listed below:

- www.Facebook.com/MarkBilton
- www.Twitter.com/MarkBilton
- www.Linkedin/in/MarkBilton
- www.YouTube.com/MarkBilton
- www.Pinterest.com/MarkBilton

Other Recommended Marketplace Ministries.

- www.MarketplaceLeaders.org

Os Hillman is president of Marketplace Leaders, an organization whose purpose is to help men and women discover and fulfill God's complete purposes through their work and to view their work as ministry. Marketplace Leaders exists to help men and women fulfill God's call on their lives by providing a *free* devotional that goes out to over a quarter of a million people all over the world and by training business leaders to see their work as a catalyst for change through training events and other ministry events.

- **www.LICC.org.uk**

LICC exists to envision and equip Christians and their churches for whole-life missionary discipleship in the world. They seek to serve them with biblical frameworks, practical resources, training, and models so that they flourish as followers of Jesus and grow as whole-life disciple-making communities. Mark Greene is one of the most articulate and effective communicators in the marketplace today.

- **www.GodatWork.org.uk**

In his book *God at Work*, Ken Costa writes about how the Christian faith should and can be lived out in day-to-day life at work. As a high-profile banker in the city of London, he considers the challenges of living out his faith at work and speaks openly of his own struggles with ambition, money, relationships, success, and failure.

By using the Biblical principles that underpin his faith and applying them to the 21st-century workplace of today, he offers practical advice on tackling the common problems familiar to many: the work-life balance, stress, ambition, failure, and disappointment.

- **www.BusinessasMissionNetwork.com**

This is the most comprehensive source of information about the Business as Mission Movement, with many links to numerous companies, resources, and articles.

- **www.EdSilvoso.com**

Ed Silvoso is one of the most effective marketplace ministers in the world, transforming many businesses and lives as he teaches comprehensively in many countries.

- **www.JohnMaxwell.com**

John Maxwell is still one of the best and most-respected experts and teachers on leadership and personal growth.

MON DAY
matters

Finding God in your workplace.

By Mark Bilton

■■■■·········■■■■■········■■■■■····■■■■■

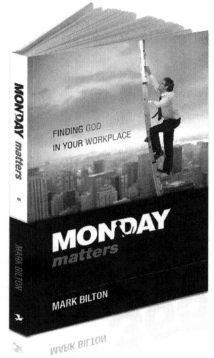

Is God really interested in my work?

There is a revolution taking place around the world. It is a realization that God is vitally, passionately, and intimately interested in the workplace. Many have embraced the biblical concept of our whole lives being impacted by God and that there is no separation between the sacred and the secular.

How do you find God in your workplace? In this book, Mark provides insights and a practical framework that lays out God's purpose for work. These lessons have been mined from real world commercial experience. Author Mark Bilton has walked with God and seen Him open doors that have taken him from the shop floor to the boardroom; from sales assistant to CEO.

Work is a vital part of His plan and purpose for us. We have been lovingly crafted, anointed, and appointed for a particular purpose. We will only reach our full potential as we recognize God's hand at work in our work.

www.MondayMatters.net